W. R. MATTHEWS:
PHILOSOPHER AND THEOLOGIAN

W. R. MATTHEWS: PHILOSOPHER AND THEOLOGIAN

by
H. P. OWEN
*Professor of Christian Doctrine
at King's College in the University of London*

UNIVERSITY OF LONDON
THE ATHLONE PRESS
1976

Published by
THE ATHLONE PRESS
UNIVERSITY OF LONDON
at 4 Gower Street London WC1
Distributed by Tiptree Book Services Ltd
Tiptree, Essex

U.S.A. and Canada
Humanities Press Inc
New Jersey

© H. P. Owen 1976

0 485 12027 5

Set in Monotype Bembo by
GLOUCESTER TYPESETTING CO LTD
Printed in Great Britain by
EBENEZER BAYLIS & SON LTD
The Trinity Press, Worcester, and London

PREFACE

The main facts of W. R. Matthews' life are these. He was born in 1881 and died in 1973. After graduating in King's College London and serving in London parishes he became Dean of King's College and Professor of the Philosophy of Religion in 1918. In 1931 he was elected Dean of Exeter and three years later Dean of St Paul's in succession to W. R. Inge. Among his many honours the chief were those of being made K.C.V.O. and C.H.

This book is not a biography. Matthews' life is amply covered in his autobiography entitled *Memories and Meanings* that was published in 1969. In the preface he admits that a defect of the book is that it tells too little of his thought. I hope to fill the gap that he, on his own admission, left. My aim is to summarize his thought (with as much quotation as possible), to place it in its historical context, and to offer an assessment of it.

The author of *The Times*' obituary wrote thus of Matthews. 'By his death the Church in England loses one of the small company of philosophical theologians of outstanding quality who have enriched its life during the last half-century.'[1] I agree. It is my hope that my exposition, even without my comments, will confirm *The Times*' verdict.

There are two further points I wish to make by way of introduction. First, Matthews is remarkably free from 'datedness'. Inevitably all writers are dated to some degree (although they are not necessarily to be dismissed on this score, for we cannot understand the present in any sphere apart from a consideration of the past). Yet although Matthews wrote against a philosophical background that may now seem old-fashioned, and although he was always concerned to communicate Christian truths in a form that would commend them to his own generation, his thought has an unusual quality of timelessness that was produced by an unusual cast of mind.

Secondly, Matthews' writings are almost invariably lucid. I have read scarcely a sentence of his that is ambiguous or obscure. He also wrote with a deceptive simplicity. I say 'deceptive' because it often conceals a learning that other writers would have revealed in the form of detailed documentation. Moreover he avoided *clichés* and jargon. He employed technical terms only when they are unavoidable. These literary qualities help to explain why he reached a wide public even when he wrote on abstract and complex topics.

Hence I endorse the following words written by the editor of the *Daily Telegraph* in an introduction to an anthology of Saturday Sermons[2] that Matthews contributed to the *Daily Telegraph* over a period of 24 years:

> The Dean was one of the most accomplished journalists of his long age. He was a formidable theological scholar, and his scholarship served not any sectarian controversy or display of learning but a perfect simplicity of language and thought. Absolute clarity, a rigorous avoidance of jargon—even the respectable jargon of the pulpit—and gentle persuasiveness were the hallmarks of his style. All journalism is, in a sense, ephemeral, and those who read these pages will doubtless see in them evidence of the special pre-occupations of the last two and a half decades. He was never a victim, however, of the shallow passion for topical 'relevance' which disfigures so much religious writing today. He saw the trials, tribulations and achievements of his own time (and he gave due weight to all three) as illustrations of the abiding state of mankind. For him, they confirmed the central truths of the Christian faith, and only in the light of those truths could the events of contemporary history be made intelligible.

Matthews wrote copiously in the form of books, articles, lectures and sermons. His most important book was *God in Christian Thought and Experience*. I shall quote almost entirely from his published works. Among the unpublished writings that he left the only one of any philosophical or theological importance is the first draft of an uncompleted book on faith: but this does not add anything of substance to his published reflections on religious epistemology. I shall sometimes refer to his works by an initial, but when I do so I shall make it clear in the first reference (e.g. by placing 'G' after the first reference to *God in Christian Thought and Experience*). In each chapter I shall first state Matthews' views and then comment on them separately.

It gives me pleasure to thank various persons and institutions. My chief debt of gratitude is to the Dean of King's College, the Reverend S. H. Evans. It was he who asked me to write this book. I am grateful to him both for initially honouring me with his request and for subsequently giving me every help in ensuring the book's publication. Next I wish to thank the following for contributing towards the cost of publication: The Dean and Chapter of St Paul's Cathedral, The Council of King's College, London, The Dean and Chapter of Exeter Cathedral, The Governing Body of Wilson's Grammar School, Camberwell. Finally I wish to thank the Board of Management of the Athlone Press for agreeing to publish the book and Miss A. M. Wyatt for typing my manuscript.

H. P. O.

CONTENTS

1	THE CONCEPT OF GOD	1
2	RELIGION AND REASON	18
3	CHRISTOLOGY AND ETHICS	46
4	CONCLUSION	70
	NOTES	77
	INDEX	83

I

The Concept of God

Matthews' views on this topic were reached only after careful attention to the teaching of those philosophers and theologians who by common consent are regarded as 'experts' and 'authorities'. I shall therefore begin with his response to patristic and scholastic teaching. The ways in which his agreement and disagreement with the Fathers and Schoolmen helped to determine his own thought will soon become apparent.

Matthews maintains that in Christian tradition Hebraic and Hellenic ideas of God have never been successfully synthesized. Whereas the Jews conceived God as a personal Creator who enters into a personal relationship with his creatures, the Greeks tended to conceive him as a non-personal and wholly transcendent Absolute. Neither the Fathers nor the Schoolmen managed to fuse these contrasting forms of theology. 'Whereas the Scholastic argument starts from abstract qualities, considered apart from the personal life in which they appear, and then arrives at an abstract notion of God, Jesus sets out from the highest human personal life, from the concrete self and its relations, and takes them as being faint shadows of the perfect but not less concrete and personal life of God.'[1]

The chief charge that Matthews brings against the Hellenic, and particularly the Platonic, element in patristic and scholastic theology is that it makes God into a wholly self-sufficient being who is not in any way affected by or involved in the joys and sorrows of mankind. This is what he says of scholasticism:

> The logical deduction is explicitly drawn that the creation of the world makes no difference to God: it cannot add to the satisfaction of the divine Experience nor could its degeneration or annihilation diminish

the fullness of the divine bliss. All the sources of God's perfect Life are found within His own being. We are here far indeed from the Biblical picture of the sons of God shouting for joy and the Creator rejoicing over all His works. It is surely a curious result of Christian philosophy that it should lead to a doctrine of God which, through anxiety to preserve His real divinity, excludes from His experience any real care for the world which He has created. In the same way, we are precluded by this philosophical conception of the nature of Deity from believing that the phrases in which religion expresses its thought about the meaning of sin and the reality of redemption have anything more than a merely metaphorical or 'economic' truth. The eternal satisfaction and self-sufficiency of God suffer no hurt through the sin of man, nor can it be increased by the turning again of the prodigal and his restoration to communion with his Creator. We are far away in this circle of ideas from the central Christian affirmation that 'there is joy in heaven over one sinner that repenteth'.[2]

At the same time Matthews acknowledges the merits of the alliance that the Fathers and Schoolmen formed between the Christian religion and Greek philosophy. 'Without this alliance', he writes, 'the Gospel could never have commended itself to the educated classes.'[3] More profoundly he praises scholasticism for its intrinsic qualities which he sums up thus:

It is in intention and inspiration profoundly Christian. It adheres to the Biblical revelation with perhaps undiscriminating loyalty, but it does not question the supreme authority of the life and words of Christ. The corporate experience of the Church has entered into its structure—perhaps again sometimes in questionable form, since it accepts the dogmatic decisions of the Councils without criticism. But with whatever imperfections this theology has grown up in an atmosphere of worship, and, at least in the case of its greatest minds, has been thought out by men whose inner life was directed towards God as the goal of all their endeavour. It is at the same time splendidly rationalist. In the form which has had the imprimatur of the Roman Church, it asserts that the existence and the fundamental attributes of God can be demonstrated by the reason unassisted by revelation. It is magnificently insistent upon the divine transcendence. In definite antagonism to any theory that the Divine is the order of the world, or the immanent reason, or the qualities of value or sublimity which the world displays, it affirms that God is 'distinct really and in essence from the world', its Source and Creator.[4]

I shall examine Matthews' own concept of God under the following topics: the personality of God, the love of God, God's perfection, his omnipotence, his omniscience, his immutability, his eternity, his impassibility, his transcendence and immanence, his creativity, his triunity.

1. PERSONALITY

Matthews attaches great importance to the belief that God is personal. The belief, he claims, has many grounds. The first ground is a moral one. 'The "values" which religion seeks to find fulfilled and sustained in the Beyond the Self are indeed recognized as no creatures of the human spirit, they are universal in claim and they are objective, but they have no existence, nor can their existence be conceived apart from personal life. A thought of God, therefore, which has expunged all tincture of anthropomorphism must decline into a concept of a being for whom no human values are real, into an unknowable ground of the universe or an order of nature.'[5] To this claim Matthews proceeds to add the facts that Jesus spoke of God in personal terms, that man is made in God's image, and that the human personality of Jesus was the supreme medium of God's self-revelation.

Later in the same book Matthews offers further grounds for belief in divine personality:

> We may now approach the personality of God with a somewhat more definite conception of the nature of the problems involved, and perhaps with a deeper appreciation of the kind of justification which may be found for the religious conviction that God is personal. The idea of God is, first, the idea of the Most Real Being. But, as we have seen, the intuition of the self is that element and moment in our experience in which we come upon that which is most unquestionably real, and that moreover from which all our concepts of reality are, in the last resort, derived. On this ground then the personality of God suggests itself as the most acceptable hypothesis. The idea of God, again, is

the idea of the Source of all other beings: the Creator. But we have seen that creation is, in our experience, a distinctive mark of personal life. The conception of a Source of being suggests the hypothesis of a Personal God. The idea of God is the idea of the Ground of unity, of the Being in whom all things cohere. But personal life is the most definite form of multiplicity in unity with which we are acquainted, and on this ground it is most reasonable to think of God as personal. Moreover, personality, as we know it, is a type of existence which bears on its face the promise of a greater perfection and a higher degree of individuality. From the very imperfect unities which our own selves present we are led to form the conception of a personal Life in which these imperfections have vanished.[6]

In order to strengthen these arguments Matthews observes that although Buddhism began as a non-theistic form of religion it became, in its Mahayana form, a theistic one. 'The significant fact about Buddhism is that it could not remain at the standpoint of Buddha. To be a religion it was compelled by an inner necessity to have personal deities, and the veneration of the Path has been absorbed in the more personal veneration of the Redeemer who discovered it.'[7]

Matthews admits that it is proper to call God 'supra-personal', and that all we need claim is that he is 'at least personal'. Yet his main emphasis is, not on the possibility that God possesses supra-personal properties, but on the fact that he possesses personal ones in a perfect mode. 'Nevertheless the Christian faith and the Christian experience are alike involved in the assertion that in the divine Life is the perfection of personality so that it is manifested in the Incarnation through the life of a perfect human Person.'[8]

2. LOVE

It is to be expected that a Christian theologian who stresses the fact of God's personality will also stress the fact of his love. And that is what we find in the case of Matthews. Yet he insists that we interpret the idea of God's love through the idea of his holiness. 'The love of God is that of the Holy One who by His act of redemption lifts man out of the condition of sin and alienation to the condition in which he is forgiven and set upon the way of sanctification. Nothing could be further from the New Testament conception of God than that of the "good fellow" of Omar, or of the deity whose *métier* it is to forgive, of the dying Heine. It is only safe to approach the doctrine of the divine Love through the doctrine of the divine Holiness.'[9] Hence 'we must not take the saying, "God is love", as if it were, in the language of logicians, a simply convertible proposition. It is not equivalent to the statement that "love is God". This remark is of some importance, for the Johannine text has sometimes been used as the support of a vague sentimentalism which loses hold of the truth that God is holy and creative Personality. God is a personal life whose fundamental quality is love, whose acts and purposes are to be interpreted in the light of this conviction. Love is not God but "*of* God".'[10]

Matthews selects two characteristics of human love at its highest. These are (in the words of P. Elmer More) 'that outreaching power of the imagination by which we grasp and make real to ourselves the being of others' and (in Matthews' own words) 'a settled will for the good of the beloved'.[11] Both characteristics are possessed by God in an infinite and perfect form to which we, as finite and sinful creatures, cannot attain.

3. PERFECTION

Matthews affirms that whereas finite beings are always pursuing ideals that they never fully actualize God is wholly perfect. 'No doctrine of God could, of course, allow that the imperfection, the contrast with the ideal, is in the Godhead itself. It would be no less absurd than blasphemous to imagine that God is trying to become better, or that one Person within the Godhead is striving for the amelioration of another.'[12] As for Anselm so for Matthews God is that than which nothing greater can be conceived (*id quo nihil maius cogitari potest*).

4. OMNIPOTENCE

Matthews adheres to the traditional view that God can do all things that are compatible with his rationality and goodness. Admittedly it is tempting to solve the problem of evil by assuming that God is confronted by hostile elements over which he does not have complete control. Matthews rejects this assumption on the ground that, according to the Christian concept of creation, all things depend on God absolutely.[13] He further maintains that the existence of evil is inevitable if God designed the world as a sphere for spiritual growth—as a 'vale of soul making' in Keats' phrase. Yet he admits that some forms of evil are not immediately explicable in this or any other way. Creation is, in Bishop Butler's words, 'a scheme imperfectly comprehended'.[14]

5. OMNISCIENCE

Matthews takes it for granted that God, as the infinite Creator, knows all that is knowable. He concentrates on the frequently discussed question whether God foreknows choices yet to be made by his human creatures. He concludes that such foreknowledge would be incompatible with the reality of free will. 'Though I may predict with some accuracy the action of a friend whom I know very well, I never imagine that my prediction is more than probable, and if I could predict with absolute certainty what my friend would do, it could only be because his actions were completely determined in advance. It seems to me that we cannot escape the same conclusion when we are considering divine Foreknowledge. If this is absolute, the course of events must be predetermined, either by the will of God or in some other way. I see no escape from the dilemma: either we must hold that all events, including acts of evil will, are determined by the will of God, or we must hold that God's foreknowledge is not absolute.'[15] Yet even if God is 'surprised' by some of the choices that his creatures make he is never baffled or frustrated by them. 'To compare the very great with the trivial, we can gain some help from the analogy of the master chess-player. He cannot foretell the moves of his unskilled opponent, and they may often cause him astonishment; but his confidence is unshaken that, whatever they may be, he can meet them and turn them to the advantage of his plan. So we may hold that there can be no thread however dark which God cannot weave into the pattern of His vast tapestry, there can be no note however discordant which cannot be taken up with the divine harmony.'[16]

6. IMMUTABILITY

That God is changeless follows from the fact that he is perfect. Matthews claims that belief in God's immutability is not merely the conclusion of a metaphysical argument; it is based on religious needs. 'The need for the Eternal rises out of the heart of the religious consciousness. The soul seeks to rest in a God who is not subject to change: it desires to find One in whom there can be "no shadow cast by turning". Unless we can be assured of this, we cannot hold the attitude of trustfulness towards Reality, or the faith that it is on the side of our deepest intuitions of value.'[17] Yet the idea of God's changelessness must be interpreted in personal terms. It must be taken to mean that God is 'One whose nature and purposes cannot alter, and who remains always consistent with himself'.[18] His immutability 'is more like the steadfastness of a good man than the unalterable properties of a triangle'.[19]

7. ETERNITY

According to classical theism (as summed up in the writings of Aquinas) to say that God is eternal is to say that he is timeless—that he exists in a single, instantaneous Now. Matthews does not reject this idea completely although he finds it 'extraordinarily difficult'.[20] His aim is to affirm the following, complementary, theses. On the one hand God must be involved in temporality at least to the extent that he knows the temporal order in its objectively real successiveness. On the other hand this knowledge does not change him (as successiveness and the knowledge of it change human creatures). 'We must attribute at least this degree of simultaneity to the divine Experience: it is not in any way at the mercy of succession. In this, on any view, it must differ from the human experience at its fullest. God is always the master of the events which enter into His life; the resources of His nature are adequate to every change, and there can be no vicissitude through which He cannot realize His will.'[21]

8. IMPASSIBILITY

The dominant view among patristic and scholastic theologians was that God cannot suffer (that is, experience pain). Matthews maintains that 'the reasons for holding that suffering enters into the divine Experience are of greater weight than those against the belief', although he also maintains that 'the suffering of God is transfigured by the vision of the travail of his soul in which is his satisfaction'.[22] He proceeds to affirm that the chief reason for ascribing pain to God is the Incarnation. 'The incarnation of the Son and His redeeming sacrifice are, for the Christian, the supreme revelation of the divine Nature. Must we not, therefore, conclude that the cross is no merely historical event, however full of influence for the future, but a sacrament of the life of God? In the sacrifice "once offered" we have, projected into time, the very heart of the divine Life and Activity. I do not see how otherwise we can present any doctrine of the atonement which does justice to the New Testament experience.'[23]

9. TRANSCENDENCE AND IMMANENCE

God is transcendent in both an ontological and an epistemological sense. He is so in the first sense by being the Creator on whom all things depend. He is so in the second sense by being the *Deus absconditus* whom no human mind can comprehend. Religion requires that his transcendence and immanence be stressed equally. 'On the one hand, a purely immanent deity turns out, in the last resort, to be undistinguishable from ourselves, and hence to be no possible object of adoration and aspiration, while conversely, a purely transcendent Deity is one with whom communion would be impossible. Either conception, in the long run, must deprive worship of its justification and prayer of its reality.'[24]

10. CREATIVITY

Matthews notes that the idea of God as one who creates the whole world out of nothing (*ex nihilo*) was a peculiarity of Christian thought in the ancient world (in contrast with Plato's view of God as a Demiurge who imposes form on pre-existent matter, Plotinian emanationism and Gnostic dualism). Moreover, the idea is essential to the Christian understanding of God's relation to the world. 'We are not parts of God, but His creatures; not phases or aspects of the Absolute, but spirits with some limited but genuine freedom to seek God or to turn away from Him. The belief in creation then safeguards the truth that all beings depend upon God as their Source and Sustainer, but, at the same time, preserves the dignity of personal spirits as self-determining agents, who are capable of receiving, in their development, the power of a "new creation" which proceeds from the same God who called them into existence.'[25]

It is important to realize that (as the end of the preceding passage states) Matthews defends the concept of creation and rejects pantheism, not only on religious grounds, but equally because pantheism is incompatible with our primary conviction that each human self is distinct and incommunicable. Thus earlier in the same book he wrote thus of Idealism (in the form presented by Gentile). 'It seems to fail the Christian theologian precisely at the point where it departs most widely from common sense. The resolution of the finite self into some very shadowy reflection or projection of the Transcendental Ego, the swallowing up of the many thinkers in the one Thinking, is plainly contrary to our *prima facie* experience. To me at least it seems that one of the most certain facts about the world is that it is experienced at different centres of consciousness and acted upon from different centres of conation. And it is equally clear that the central Christian view of God and the world is opposed to such an absorption of the finite self.'[26]

The distinctive element in Matthews' concept of creation consists in his repeated assertion that God is not self-sufficient but that creation is necessary for the fulfilment of his being. Matthews gives several reasons for this assertion (which he admits is a departure from classical theism). His basic reason is that the very idea of personality involves the pursuit of ideals and the existence of a sphere in which they are not yet realized. Yet this sphere cannot exist within God himself; for he is perfect. 'If therefore we hold that God is personal, we are forced to the conclusion that He finds in the created world, or in the creatures, the sphere, distinct from Himself, in which His ideal ends are to be attained. Apart from that created order with its imperfection and its capacity for progress He could not be personal.'[27]

Matthews gives two other reasons. First, to say that God has a purpose implies that he feels a need that only the fulfilment of this purpose can satisfy.[28] Secondly, the idea of God's self-sufficiency contradicts the New Testament's descriptions of his love and grace. I have already quoted Matthews for this view in connection with his objections to scholasticism. Here is another passage. 'The gospel of the grace of God is certainly not the message that God is self-sufficient and incapable of want or desire. It is almost the opposite of that—it is the proclamation of the love of God, which seeks me and will not be satisfied until I return to Him. Our hearts are restless until they find rest in God; but is there no corresponding truth about the divine experience? "We love Him because he first loved us"—His heart is restless until we find rest in Him.'[29]

Because the act of creation is a necessary expression of God's nature it must be eternal. 'Unless therefore we are willing to attribute to God a merely "interim" personality, a selfhood which begins with creation and ends with the consummation of the present order we shall be compelled to hold that the activity of creation is eternal.'[30] Matthews quotes Origen in support. This does not mean that either our universe or any other universe is eternal. It means only that there must be some created being of some kind.

II. TRIUNITY

In his *God in Christian Thought and Experience* Matthews devotes a whole chapter to the doctrine of the Trinity. He begins by stressing its novelty. It is not found in the Old Testament. Also the Plotinian Triad is no true parallel (for whereas the members of the latter are co-eternal they are not co-equal). The ground of the doctrine lies in the apostolic experience of Christ as the incarnate

Lord, and of the Spirit as one who mediates the life of Christ to believers. Moreover, we cannot be content with a merely 'economic' Trinity for two reasons. First, unless God were essentially triune he would be, in his ultimate nature as a solitary and unrevealed Absolute, unknowable. Secondly, the idea that there is in God an inner core that transcends his triune revelation conflicts with the belief (to which, as we have seen, Matthews adheres) that God's self-manifestation in the world is an essential element in his Godhood.

The Trinity is the archetype of selfhood. It constitutes the removal of those imperfections that characterize selfhood in its human form. In every human self there is a discrepancy between the 'I' and the 'me'; but there is no such discrepancy in God. In order to understand Matthews' thought here one must refer back to the preceding chapter. There he argued that 'I' can never have an adequate knowledge of myself ('me') because the latter is partly formed by external factors. 'The acts and impulses, which, retained in memory, form the data of our conception of the self are, to a large extent, to an indefinite extent, modified by circumstances which are beyond our power to influence or radically alter. In so far as our activity is determined by the environment we are debarred from a complete knowledge of ourselves. The "me" which I contemplate is not simply the creation of the Ego but the resultant of the central activity of the self modified by the circumstances in which that activity has been exercised.'[31] Yet this does not apply to God; for nothing in his nature is formed by factors outside himself. Hence 'in the divine experience, and in no other experience, can the "me", the self known, be the "express image", the adequate representation, of the "I", the knower'.

Matthews then considers the question whether there are any *a priori* arguments for supposing that there must be real and permanent distinctions within the Godhead. He dismisses the view that these must exist because if God is love he must have an object for his love; for God always has such an object in the created order. However, Matthews maintains that such distinctions must be posited on the ground that a perfect personality must have an *adequate* object for his love, and that for God this object must be divine. 'The completely personal being, the being in whom personal existence achieves the highest quality, must be a being for whom there exists a responsive object adequate to himself. Once again we are led to the thought of a plurality within the unity of the Godhead, we come back again to the conception of a reciprocal relatedness of active and conscious centres.'[32] But Matthews also holds that it is impossible to prove that the members of the Godhead must be three and not two or more than three.

The importance that Matthews attached to the doctrine of the Trinity may be judged from the following words that he wrote in an essay re-published towards the end of the Second World War:

> The doctrine of the Trinity has sometimes been called the distinctive feature of Christianity. There is truth in this, though the first triumphs of the Church were gained before the doctrine was clearly formulated and expressed. Into the subtleties of the theological questions which arose in connexion with this dogma we shall not here enter, nor do they affect in any serious degree the faith of the ordinary Christian. It is, however, important to observe that the doctrine is not a piece of gratuitous speculation which theologians who had nothing better to do have tacked on to the Gospel. A practical purpose is behind it; nothing less than to guard the essentials of the Christian faith. It is intended to preserve the right to offer worship to Jesus Christ and to the Holy Spirit as divine, while at the same time retaining unimpaired the belief that there is only one God, which the Church inherited from the Jews. The doctrine of the Trinity was the way by which the Church avoided Polytheism. The adoration of Christ, which was the centre of the Church's life, might have issued in a belief that He was a second God beside the Father; that it did not do so is due to the fact that the leaders of the Church, under the guidance as Christians believe of the Holy Spirit, stated and thought out the doctrine of the Trinity which they believed, and with justice, could be found in germ in the New Testament. The dogma was not an addition to Scripture, but an explanation of what Scripture implied.[33]

Matthews has the support of many twentieth-century theologians in holding that the Fathers and Schoolmen incompletely fused Biblical and Greek modes of thought. Yet let us note his moderation. He does not dismiss patristic thought as a corruption of primitive Christianity. On the contrary he always speaks of the Fathers and the Creeds with respect. Also he commends scholasticism for its rationality, its comprehensiveness, and its recognition of divine transcendence. In fact his only concrete objection to scholasticism is that it describes God as a self-sufficient being.

I shall proceed to comment on those elements in Matthews' concept of God that are most significant both in themselves and in their relation to twentieth-century thought.

Matthews' stress on God's personal character has many parallels in this century. One thinks of Buber's claim that our relation with God is of an 'I-Thou', not an 'I-It', kind. Also Bultmann's whole project of 'demythologization' was based on the conviction that faith takes the form of an 'encounter' with the Word. Matthews' distinctive contribution here is double. First, he is determined to avoid anthropomorphism; and so he is content to say that God is not less than personal (according to our understanding of personality). Secondly, he does not merely assert that God is personal; he also gives reasons for the assertion. And I find these convincing.

Matthews' further insistence on the Johannine affirmation that 'God is love' may not seem to require comment. Yet the most profound truths can degenerate into unexamined clichés. Matthews reminds us of two facts. First, God's love is a *holy* love. It is removed as far as possible from indulgence or sentimentality. Secondly, although we can say 'God is love' we cannot reverse the proposition and say 'Love is God'. Yet some forms of radical theology in recent years have come perilously near to this reversal.

Matthews' treatment of God's perfection and immutability reveals the search for a 'middle way' that characterizes much of his thought. On the one hand he retains belief in these divine attributes. Hence he implicitly rules out Hegel's idea of an Absolute that develops itself through historical events, Hartshorne's 'dipolar' concept of God as one who is constantly surpassing himself in one aspect of his nature, and John Macquarrie's view that

God is characterized by 'becoming' as well as 'being'.[34] To this extent he sides firmly with classical theism. On the other hand he maintains that in order to reconcile belief in these attributes with the Biblical portrait of God we must re-interpret them. The idea of God's perfection must be separated from the idea of his self-sufficiency, and the idea of his changelessness must be expressed in terms of his personal self-consistency.

A similar attempt at mediation may be discerned in Matthews' approach to the divine attributes of eternity and impassibility. On the former he held on the one hand that the identification of God's 'eternity' with 'timelessness' is dubitable, but on the other hand that even though God is temporal in so far as he knows events in their objectively real succession (so that he does not foreknow free human choices), he exercises a complete mastery over all events. Again, Matthews held that although God suffers in response to the sins and sorrows of his creatures his sufferings are transfigured by his joy.

The fundamental point at which Matthews shows his affinity with traditional theism is his adherence to the doctrine of creation. He rightly affirmed that from the beginning Christianity has been characterized by belief in God as one who created the world *ex nihilo* and on whom the world totally depends. His own adherence to the doctrine was determined further by his sense of divine transcendence—a sense sharpened by his admiration for Otto's *The Idea of the Holy* and by his conviction that pantheism is incompatible with the integrity of human selfhood. The importance of Matthews' continual insistence on the doctrine of creation is double.

First, Matthews here dissociates himself from the two influential movements in twentieth-century thought that I have already mentioned—namely, Hegelianism and process theology. Both can be called, in varying ways, panentheistic. According to the first the world is the self-expression of absolute Spirit. According to the second God, like Plato's *Demiurge*, does not create the world; he merely imposes form on antecedently given flux. Moreover according to Whitehead the world 'creates' God (by contributing to his consequent nature) quite as much as God 'creates' the world (by imparting structure and vision to it).[35]

Secondly, Matthews' firm assent to the doctrine of creation meant that although he was prepared to modify the concepts of divine perfection and immutability he could not abandon them. He could not agree that the world helps to create God and augment his perfection. Nor could he agree that God, through his involvement with the world, actualizes a form of being that was before only potential. Similarly he was obliged to hold that even if God suffers his sufferings are transformed by the joy that is necessarily his as the Lord of a creation over which he has complete control.

Furthermore Matthews sees clearly that the distinguishing element in the Christian view of God is the doctrine of the Trinity. Although he is in many respects closer to Schleiermacher than he is to Barth he is closer to the latter than he is to the former in holding that the doctrine belongs to the essence of the Christian faith. Also I think he gives good grounds for affirming that the doctrine is unparalleled; that a merely 'economic' (as against 'essential') form of trinitarianism is insufficient; and that God's triune life is the perfection of selfhood.

I shall now consider the three points at which Matthews diverges from classical theism. The only major point is on the question of God's self-sufficiency. This divergence determines both his chief objection to scholasticism and his view that differentiation within the Godhead is required in order that God may have, not merely *an* object, but an *adequate* object of his love. In maintaining that God needs the world Matthews was in the company of many distinguished thinkers of his period.[36] Yet I do not find his arguments convincing, and I think he was inconsistent. Why is it necessary to affirm that personality involves the pursuit of ideals? After all even creatures will cease from this pursuit when they attain their final rest in heaven. Moreover Matthews' view involves an antinomy that E. L. Mascall has expressed thus. 'Either God will ultimately achieve his ideals, in which case he will thenceforth cease to be personal, or else he will remain forever personal at the cost of never achieving his ideals.'[37] Furthermore, the idea of God's self-sufficiency is not incompatible with the idea of his love. On the contrary because only God is self-sufficient only his love is wholly altruistic. In every human act of love the lover needs the object of his love for the fulfilment of his being. The infinite nature of God's love is shown in the overflowing goodness whereby he created a world of which he has no need. Finally, if, as Matthews asserts, the Father has an adequate object of love in the Son he must be self-sufficient in his personal nature.

The other two points at which Matthews diverges from classical theism concern God's impassibility and omniscience. I do not intend to discuss these attributes or Matthews' interpretation of them.[38] I merely wish to offer two comments.

First, if we endorse Matthews' interpretation we can do so without endangering belief in the other divine attributes I have examined. Thus even if we hold that God suffers we can consistently also hold that he is self-sufficient and immutable. Such sufferings would be wholly vicarious and self-imposed; they would be expressions of the same altruistic love that is God's only motive for creation; and (as Matthews stresses) they would be immediately transfigured by God's joy. Similarly even if we admit that God does not know free acts of human choice before they have been made the admission would not conflict with belief in his omniscience and omnipotence. It would not conflict with belief in the former; for even God can know only those things that are knowable. It would not conflict with the latter; for God can assimilate all human choices to his sovereign will.

Secondly, these points are secondary. They involve a further interpretation of divine properties in which all Christians believe. Thus all believe that God loves, cares for, and pities us infinitely. Also all believe that he knows everything that is knowable, and that his knowledge is suffused by his love. Whether his love involves suffering and whether his knowledge of his creatures takes a timeless form are further questions. Perhaps too they are questions that no finite mind can answer with certainty. In any case all we need to know is that God is loving and omniscient.

Agnosticism concerning the experiential modes of his love and knowledge is religiously tolerable. I think Matthews would have agreed.

Matthews' only serious divergence from traditional theism, then, is his denial of God's self-sufficiency. In conclusion I wish, not to stress my criticisms of him here, but to state two points that (even if I am right) stand in his favour. First, admittedly there *appears* to be a conflict between scholastic affirmations of God's self-sufficiency and the Biblical portrait of him as a loving Father who seeks the good of his children. This appearance is intensified by the fact that scholastic terminology is apt to evoke the idea of Aristotle's God who, wrapt in self-contemplation, is indifferent to the world. Secondly, although Matthews exhibits an affinity with Hegelianism and process thought in his denial of God's self-sufficiency his adherence to the Christian doctrines of creation and the Trinity prevents him from subscribing to the distinctive tenets of either of these two schools.

2

Religion and Reason

Matthews devoted much thought to the analysis of religion in general and the Christian religion in particular. The substance of his thought here is contained in his *God in Christian Thought and Experience*. Hence my initial references will be to this work.

Matthews begins by commending Schleiermacher for treating the religious impulse 'as an inherent and necessary quality of human consciousness which normally develops along with the mind itself'.[1] Yet he brings three objections against Schleiermacher's definition of religion as 'a feeling of absolute dependence'. First, although Schleiermacher included an element of awareness or perception in 'feeling' 'we cannot absolve him altogether from the charge of neglecting the part of reason and conscience in religious development'.[2] Secondly he interprets man's relation to God in too passive a way. Religion consists in co-operation with God as well as dependence on him. Thirdly Schleiermacher's definition omits the feelings of reverence and awe—feelings that Otto stressed in his identification of religions experience with a sense of the 'numinous'. Nevertheless, Matthews holds, Otto no less than Schleiermacher erred in separating religion from other manifestations of the human spirit. 'It is significant that neither of them gives us a wholly satisfactory account of how moral values and intellectual judgments come to be so closely associated with a form of the spirit with which, on their hypothesis, they have no necessary connection.'[3]

Matthews then suggests that religion can be defined as the sense or intuition of 'the Beyond which is akin'. This intuition reaches its fulfilment in the mystical theism exemplified by Augustine. His aim was 'to rise, in an experience which transcends discursive thought, to a Being who is indeed far other than himself, and yet a Being in whom he knows that he will find his completion and his home'.[4]

Religion, moreover, seeks to satisfy two needs: the need for unity and the need for the substantiation of value. On the first Matthews notes that, although only monotheism can finally unify our total experience, a provisional unification is provided by polytheism in so far as 'the world as interpreted by polytheism is a more coherent thing than the world not interpreted at all'.[5] The second need is to be assured that our moral judgments 'are not mere passing preferences but grounded in reality'.[6] This need also is completely satisfied only by monotheism (in the form of belief in God as one who exemplifies moral values to an absolute degree). Moreover, religion expresses a need for redemption (although the latter is differently conceived by different religions).[7]

Matthews concludes his preliminary survey by insisting that the sense of God is not to be attributed to a special faculty or limited to a spiritual *élite*:

> The view of the general character of man's experience of God which has been presented in this chapter has a consequence which we cannot pass over in silence. If we have rightly described it, religion cannot be regarded as a specialized activity. It is certainly a distinct form of the spiritual life and is not to be resolved into morality or art or philosophy; but it is not the product of a separate faculty in the individual nor is it the peculiar prerogative of a special type of human being. It is native to the developed human consciousness. The recent interest in the lives and writings of 'mystics' and the cult of the 'religious genius' have been wholly beneficial in that they have drawn attention to a type of human faculty which had been misunderstood and have emphasized the power of the religious motive in minds of exceptional character; but there is a danger lest this type of religious thought should tend to suggest that religion itself depends upon the possession of a rare combination of qualities. It may be, too, that to judge religion by its specialists is likely to give us a distorted conception of its nature. Religion, in our view, is the completion of the other forms of the life of the spirit, the climax towards which they tend, so that each of them, when intense and full, passes over into religion.[8]

The Christian religion is distinguished from other religions by the historical events on which it is based and by the ways in which these events have influenced Christians throughout the history of the Church. The primary event is Christ himself—but Christ as the object, not the subject, of religious faith. 'Historical Christianity is not the religion of Jesus but the religion which centres upon the Person of Jesus.'[9] It does not consist merely in imitating Christ as a man who perfectly exemplified those spiritual and moral virtues that constitute the ideal of the religious life. It consists in sharing the life of Christ as the incarnate Son of God. The Pauline and Johannine writings 'declare without possibility of question that the new life, the new experience of God, which is at the heart of the Christian gospel as it was preached to the pagan world, is something quite different from a following of a human example however perfect: it is the participation in a personal Life which continues and which is divine'.[10]

Christian faith comprises three elements. The first is the experience of God's love and power incarnate in Christ. This is the 'given' of theology. The second element is the New Testament of which Matthews writes that 'it is at once the foundation and the solvent of Christian doctrine; the source from which it springs and the source also of its continual refashioning'.[11] The third element 'is the philosophical—the intellectual presuppositions and concepts which have, to a considerable degree, determined the form of the theological system'.[12]

Matthews continually affirmed that belief in God must always be based on experience. We cannot demonstrate God's existence and character by a logically coercive proof. We can believe in them only by a logically non-demonstrative intuition of their reality. Matthews made this epistemologically final point in an essay in which he sought to sum up the nature of Christian belief in God. 'Reason', he wrote, 'is not so much the instrument for the discovery of truth as the faculty by which we test alleged truth'. He went on to observe that in ordinary, secular, life experience, not reason, is determinative. He gave as an example our knowledge of other selves. 'We firmly believe that our fellows exist in the same way as we do long before our reason raises the question. We know it, as we say, "by experience". The same is true of religion. 'The belief in God depends, in the last resort, on experience, on what has been called "revelation"; but it is, in this respect, in the same position as the other beliefs on which we act in complete confidence every day.'[13]

Matthews expanded this view as follows in a paper he gave to the Society for the Study of Theology:

> I suggest that we make a mistake when we regard scientific knowledge as the model of knowledge to which all other types of knowing should conform so far as they are able. No doubt, most of us would deny that we held any such opinion, but the pressure of the scientific age is on us all, and we all succumb at times to the prevailing view that scientific knowledge is the ideal and would be glad to think that our theological statements had the respectability of scientific conclusions; but at the centre of our theology there is another kind of knowing, or so we assert, without which all our theology would be castles in the air. This knowing is of a different type. It is one in which the knower tends to become like what he contemplates: it is a kind of knowing in which subject and object interpenetrate, where, as it were, the knower reaches out to grasp the object, or the object reaches out to grasp the subject. When St. Paul cries, 'That I may know Him and the power of His resurrection,' he does not mean that he may know objectively that Christ rose from the dead and is assured that this is a true statement, though that is included as a subordinate element. He means that he may know the reality of the risen life by being part of it. And when he and others have, in some degree, come to know God or, what is the same thing, to be known of Him, they do not mean primarily that they have a well-founded conviction that the proposition 'God exists' is true, though that is included, but that they are partakers of the divine nature.[14]

However, although Matthews assigned primacy to experience in the life of faith he also held that reason is indispensable in the following ways.

(1) Reason is required in order to assess the truth-claims inherent in religion. Here the best statement of Matthews' views is contained in a published lecture entitled *Reason in Religion*:[15]

No-one who cares to keep in touch with facts can deny that illusion and error are rife in human thinking and belief, and there are many asserted revelations which conflict with one another. When two irreconcilable words professing to be of God are presented to us, we are driven back upon our own reason to decide between them. The scorn which the Barthians pour upon the attempt to establish the validity of revelation on grounds of reason seems to leave us with nothing but a subjective basis for faith. We shall not question the need for the testimony of the Holy Spirit, but does not the rejection of all appeal to reason in favour of this testimony suggest a curiously narrow view of the activity of the Spirit? Is, then, the reason, with its thirst for truth, not one of the manifestations of the Spirit? The method which has, on the whole, been adopted by Catholic theology is surely more in harmony with the real and complex situation. According to that theology, it can be shown that a divine revelation is to be expected; there is reason for supposing that, if God exists, He would reveal Himself; further, the marks of a revelation can be considered and, finally, it can be argued that the Christian revelation bears the marks by which it can be recognised as the supreme revelation compared with all others. I do not say that these lines of thought have been successfully pursued, or that the answers which we are given in the traditional theology are satisfactory; indeed, I am sure that they are not, and that the whole problem of revelation needs re-thinking, but I hold that the outline of the argument is sound.[16]

(2) Matthews always urged the necessity of formulating religious experience in doctrines. Hence in a work that he wrote as early as 1923 he affirmed that although we must interpret the idea of revelation primarily in terms of God's personal self-disclosure through and to human persons the role of dogma is, though secondary, indispensable. He put the point ecclesiastically thus:

We may, perhaps, dare to see a justification here, and even a way of reconciliation, for the Protestant and Catholic types of Christianity. Each has dwelt upon a necessary aspect of the life of a revealed religion. The Protestant insisting on the responsibility of the individual and the supreme importance of the inner life of the soul, as against all systems of doctrine, or tradition, or church order, has seized upon the truth that revelation is essentially not the communication of truths about

God, but the self-disclosure of God in personal life, and that its purpose is not primarily to teach correct theology, but to propagate an experience. But the Catholic has not been wrong in dwelling upon the need for the Church and its doctrines and traditions, for it is normally through the community and its institutions that the revelation can become available for the mass of mankind.[17]

(3) Matthews attached the highest importance to natural theology. This will be the subject of the next section.

In the course of his many writings Matthews considers all the main arguments for the existence of God. Before examining his accounts of them in detail I shall state his view of their general nature. He maintains that the theistic proofs (or at least some of them), though not capable of demonstrating God's existence with logical certainty, make belief in him 'highly probable' by showing that theism is the most satisfactory 'hypothesis' for interpreting the universe. Thus in 1920 he wrote that 'the arguments still have value, since they tend to support one kind of hypothesis and to rule out others',[18] and that they establish God's existence 'with a high degree of probability'.[19] Later, in 1944, he affirmed that 'we may perhaps think of belief in God as one of the hypotheses which have been suggested for solving a part of the riddle of the universe',[20] and that the theistic proofs endow the belief 'with a very high degree of probability'.[21]

Matthews fully recognizes the uniqueness of the God-hypothesis in the following passage that occurs in a paper he gave on 'The Aims and Scope of the Philosophy of Religion':

The hypothesis, in this case, is not strictly analogous with hypothesis as employed in the scientific method, because the God-hypothesis, if the term may be allowed, is not an hypothesis to explain a limited set of phenomena, or to solve some definite problem, but an hypothesis to explain the whole of phenomena. Further, we must remember that the hypothesis of God is, as we have seen, not one which we invent *ad hoc*. We find it, nor can we be indifferent towards it. It comes to us with the weight of centuries of human thought and emotion behind it and we cannot disguise from ourselves the fact that our choice to adhere or not to adhere to it is not only a matter of intellectual satisfaction but may be a choice between life and death, or at least between hope and despair.[22]

To the objection that the God of religion is no mere hypothesis Matthews replies as follows:

> I remember the indignation with which one of the most respected preachers of our time rejected the idea of a 'hypothetical God' when I put forward the conception in *Studies in Christian Philosophy*. His feeling is comprehensible. He was considering the matter from the standpoint of a profound religious experience; and from that point of view, God is no hypothesis but the supreme Reality, in comparison with Whom all else is fleeting and uncertain. When we worship God He is to us certainly not a mere hypothesis. But we must sometimes, as Bishop Butler says, 'sit down in a cool hour' and reflect upon the logical basis of our faith and worship. When we do this, we cannot avoid recognizing that our belief in God is one possible way of thinking of the universe and can be compared with other possible ways. No degree of mystical assurance can set us free from the necessity of meeting the challenge to show that ours is a better way, or perhaps the only satisfactory way.[23]

Furthermore Matthews admits that this view of theism as an explanatory hypothesis or postulate presupposes that the universe is ultimately intelligible. The truth of this presupposition cannot be rationally demonstrated. It must be accepted by an act of faith. Yet this act is one that we habitually perform in our quest for secular knowledge. 'The intelligibility of the world is an act of faith, but one which we cannot help making. On it is based not only all science but all knowledge of any kind. This faith in intelligibility is not "proved" by the success of science in its researches, since the postulate is assumed in every scientific investigation, but we may at least hold that it is supported and confirmed. If we generalise this assumption it leads to the postulate that "the universe can present no intrinsic inexplicability for thought". It is of course true that the complete attainment of intelligibility is not achieved and probably within finite time cannot be achieved, but it is a process which never ceases. The "brute fact" is never accepted as unanalysable'.[24]

Matthews summed up his attitude to all the main theistic proofs in his contribution to *The Christian Faith*.[25] He finds the ontological argument unconvincing (although he is unwilling to reject it finally). He accepts the cosmological argument according to which God as an infinite and necessary being is postulated as the only adequate Ground of the finite and contingent order. This argument, he says, 'lies at the root of all constructive thought'. On the teleological argument—the argument that the appearance of design in the universe compels us to postulate a cosmic Designer—he observes that although for some time after the acceptance of the Darwinian theory of evolution it was under a cloud, it can still be presented in a cogent form. Finally reflection on moral experience leads us to postulate God as an absolute Good who is 'the norm and source of all values'.

The teleological and moral arguments are those to which Matthews devoted most attention. I shall first deal with his discussion of the moral argument. I have chosen this order because I think it helps to exhibit both the development and the coherence of Matthews' thought.

Matthews formulated the moral argument in his first major work, *Studies in Christian Philosophy*. His premiss is that morality is *sui generis*; it cannot be reduced to non-moral terms. Thus 'the good' cannot be equated with 'what is of survival-value in the course of evolution'. So far Matthews agrees with G. E. Moore. Yet, unlike Moore, he wishes to draw a theistic inference from the moral consciousness. His argument runs thus. Moral ideals are objective; they are 'given' to us, and are not merely matters of subjective taste or preference. But if the moral ideal is to be objective and still be an ideal it must exist as a perfect concept in a divine Mind. 'It seems clear, therefore, that to conceive the moral ideal as having objective reality and at the same time as being an ideal, we shall be compelled to think of it as a completely conceived but as yet unrealised purpose: as a mental content which is distinct from the existing order. In other words, we are led to postulate a transcendent teleology, a purposive Intelligence which is not identical with the actual world.'[26]

Matthews is anxious not to commit a theological version of the 'naturalistic fallacy' by construing God's will as a purely transcendent and inscrutable *fiat*. God's law must be understood as the law of one's own being and so as being wholly congruous with all that is true in Kant's concept of moral autonomy. Hence he says of Christian theism that 'with its doctrine of the immanent Word or Reason, it enjoins us to hold that the apprehension whereby we discern the Good is the reflection of the Divine knowledge, and that the will whereby we attempt to realise the Good is not unrelated with the will whereby God seeks to realise His own end'.[27]

Finally Matthews contends that the goal of morality, the *Summum Bonum*, can be ultimately interpreted only as a community of persons under the rule of a holy God. This end 'requires perfected intercourse between all finite persons, and this is impossible so long as they remain finite, and equally impossible if they become infinite'.[28] This antinomy is resolved by theism. 'For Theism holds that there is a great Focus and Centre of spirits, a Mind and Character wide and pure enough to engage the love of all persons, in loving whom we love all that is worthy of affection in all finite beings. It holds that the highest blessedness for the individual is, not to be absorbed or abolished in Him, but to reach a state of will and affection in which God can be said to be living in the finite self. If this hypothesis were true the realisation of the Social End would be possible, not indeed in the precise form which we were led to give to it when we considered a purely human society, but still in its essential features. The theistic hypothesis allows us to conceive the possibility of a perfected intercourse which is all-embracing, including all persons, and which, at the same time, preserves and perfects their individual being.'[29]

Throughout his philosophical career Matthews was even more interested in the teleological argument. He was always convinced that only theism can explain, or make sense of, the evolutionary process. Thus both in his *Studies in Christian Philosophy* and in his *The Christian Experience of God* he maintained that evolution cannot be explained in terms of 'mechanistic' causality, a 'vita principle' or mere 'emergence' of the higher from the lower. But for a full statement of his view we must turn to his *The Purpose of God*. All my references for the remainder of this section will be to this book.

Matthews begins by stating his attitude to all the main theistic proofs. He accepts Kant's rejection of the ontological argument on the ground that it treats 'existence' as a predicate. More generally he affirms that both the Anselmic and the Cartesian forms of the argument involve an illegitimate leap from thought to reality. Nevertheless, Matthews maintains, every claim to knowledge rests on the ontological assumptions that 'there is an objective reality which is not merely my own experience' and that 'this objective reality is knowable'.[30] He further holds that the ontological argument can be represented in the following form: 'if there is any truth there is absolute truth, and if there is absolute truth there is absolute reality'.[31]

Matthews then affirms that the cosmological argument, though not constituting a logically inexorable demonstration, points to God as one whose existence must be postulated in order to account for the existence of a contingent world. Matthews rejects Kant's view that the category of 'cause' is applicable only to phenomena. The category, he holds, applies to 'things in themselves'. He further appeals to Whitehead in support of his claim that 'we do not, as Hume and most later philosophers tended to suppose, first have perceptions and then unite them together by the category of causation; on the contrary we perceive the causal efficacy, which is more original even than the "percepts" '.[32] Finally if God is the Ground of the world's existence we can infer that he possesses 'eminently' all those qualities that the world exhibits in a finite mode. The teleological argument, Matthews affirms, 'is properly regarded as an extension and elaboration of the cosmological'.[33]

In chapter two Matthews states the essence of the teleological argument thus. 'There are, in truth, two distinct stages in every teleological argument for Theism, though they are not always definitely marked by those who use such arguments. In the first place, it is imperative to establish the actual presence of teleological process in the world, to point to purposiveness in events; this task would be more accurately described, however, as the need to sustain the thesis that the teleological principle is a legitimate, or better, a necessary one. In the second place, comes the duty of showing that no other ground for this principle is fully adequate except a transcendent and purposive Mind.'[34] He insists that there is no contradiction between efficient, or even 'mechanical', and final causes. 'Leibniz brought out more clearly than any previous thinker the truth that there is no inconsistency between explanation by efficient cause and explanation by final cause; in fact, that a system interrelated by efficient and even "mechanical" causes may nevertheless be throughout teleological. Of course, Aristotle no less acknowledges the universal sway of both types of causation, and even Francis Bacon, who is sometimes credited with having banished final causes altogether on the ground that "like virgins consecrated to God" they are barren, insisted upon the need for final causes in metaphysics.'[35]

Matthews proceeds to admit that there are two *a priori* elements in the teleological argument—two presuppositions that we do not derive from the facts themselves. The first is that we have a real knowledge of values, and the second is that the world is intelligible. Matthews further admits that the argument involves the use of analogy in so far as it implies that nature can be understood by comparison with our own experience of intentional action. But he observes that even the ascription of efficient causes to nature (without any reference to God) 'springs from our own experience that we can change the outer world by effort',[36] and that the argument need not involve the use of crude analogies (such as the idea of a celestial watch-maker).

Matthews then examines some objections that have been brought against the teleological argument. He begins with Hume's suggestion that 'given a finite number of particles or units of any kind in an infinite time, it is probable that every possible combination of those units would take place, and among them would be the present universe whose order strikes us as supernatural'.[37]

Matthews holds that this suggestion is self-stultifying in so far as it is inapplicable to the particles themselves. 'If the particles or units which, by hypothesis, constitute this world and any possible world are not determinate in their properties, unless they either do not change at all or change only in accordance with a determinate law, there is no sense in saying that they are finite in number; there is, in fact, no sense in saying that they are units at all. In any case, a unit which may vary indefinitely may be said to have a kind of infinity of possibilities in itself, and a collection of such units would not be a finite number of units.'[38] Matthews then considers an evolutionary version of the same idea. According to this the world has acquired its present order by a fortuitous action of 'natural causes'. Matthews replies as follows. 'There can be no natural selection of nature; any materialist or mechanical theory of evolution must seek for the causes of evolution in the reaction of the evolving thing with the environment; but nature as a whole has no environment; it *is* the environment. Therefore the conception of evolution within nature precludes us from holding that nature as such evolves.'[39]

Matthews next considers the objection that the dysteleological elements in the universe render the teleological argument incapable of proving the existence of only one supernatural being who is the perfect Creator of all that is. He admits that such a proof is impossible. Yet he rejects dualism on the ground that a conflict between good and evil powers presupposes the existence of a universe they have in common. 'But this common system of things is the problem which we are concerned to elucidate. We have still to ask the explanation of its existence, and though we might think of the world as the scene of a conflict between Ormuzd and Ahriman, or between God and the devil, we should need to postulate a higher God who created and sustained the conditions which enabled them to fight.'[40]

In chapter four Matthews presents his own form of the teleological argument. This is based on the fact of the evolution of mind from matter. This fact cannot be explained by an appeal to 'natural selection'; for 'selection' implies the existence of 'variations' that can be 'selected'. In any case mind is a variation that cannot be explained in terms of its antecedent state. 'There are, however, some "variations" which are so obviously new beginnings in development that they cannot properly be described as variations in the ordinary sense. They are "mutations" which mark the starting-point of a fresh type of development. Life and mind are in no sense modifications of what was already there; they cannot be compared, for example, with the elongation of the neck of the giraffe. A living being is being of a new kind, and so, still more evidently, is a thinking being.'[41] It is equally useless to invoke the concept of 'emergent evolution'. 'The case of "emergence" can be summed up in a sentence: it is a good description but no explanation. Undoubtedly life and mind do occur in the course of evolution, and it is impossible to conceive them as mere resultants of the non-living or the non-mental, produced by causes which are at work in the inorganic world. But to state the fact does not explain it. The problem which Theism professes to solve is really there.'[42]

Furthermore, if we postulate a cosmic Mind for the emergence of human minds in the course of evolution we must also postulate it for the existence of the body. 'Even if we admitted, for the sake of argument, that my living body may have been produced by "the endless shuffling and reshuffling of merely material factors", we have still to ask how it is that the body is adapted to our mental life in so intricate a manner. How is it that the thoughts find a material system, the body, so adapted to them that they can be expressed in gesture, speech, and writing?'[43] Matthews then quotes with approval the following words from G. F. Stout's *Mind and Matter*. 'My mental agency is possible only through an immensely complex system of conditions pre-adjusted to it. These conditions themselves arise out of the previous course of events in the material world, carried backward into the indefinite past before there was any living matter, and carried forward into my present bodily movements. We cannot interpret one essentially dependent part of this continuous process as implying mental agency and yet refuse to interpret on the same principle the whole which includes it. There is a vast multitude of facts not only analogous to each other, inasmuch as they present teleological order, but interwoven in one context. By assuming mental agency in nature as well as in human and animal life, we can bring them in spite of diversity under one principle, and if this principle is rejected there is no other which will cover the facts.'[44]

However, a frequently urged objection is that even if we are compelled to postulate a cosmic Designer the existence of evil prevents us from attributing goodness to him. Matthews replies thus. The apprehension of values is an essential element in human mentality, and these cannot be explained in terms of their biological 'survival-power'. Therefore if we regard God as the origin of mind in the evolutionary process we must regard him as the origin of values also. 'Now we know nothing of any mind which is essentially different from our mind, nor if we did should we have any ground for calling it "mind". If, then, we find reason to believe that there is directive mind in nature, it must have the fundamental characteristics of mind in us. But we discover that it is an inseparable attribute of mind, as we know it, to be appreciative and creative of value.'[45] And so we arrive at the idea of a God who is, not only powerful and wise, but also good.

Finally, Matthews maintains that there is no discrepancy between the cosmic teleology he has advocated and the belief that Christ, as the incarnate Word, has established a wholly new creation.

Primitive Christianity spoke of Christians as 'the new race', and thought of Christ as the inauguration of a new creation. This conception, which at first sight seems to be at variance with a teleological view of the world, because it suggests a sudden break of continuity, is not really in disharmony with the teleological view as such, but only with one of its special forms. The opinion that a purpose can be discerned in the development of life does not necessarily imply that this purpose must be achieved always by minute gradations and slow evolution. There may be jumps, mutations, new beginnings. The emergence of life itself and still more that of mind and self-consciousness are the coming into being of totally new kinds of existence and are the starting-points of evolutionary processes of a type essentially different in character and mode of operation from that which preceded them. It is, therefore, quite consistent with what we know of the evolution of life that a new type of living should come out of the older and lower, but should be in its quality discontinuous with what went before.[46]

This, then, is the substance of Matthews' reflections on religion and natural theology. There are, however, two further topics on which I must comment.

First, in 1966 Matthews produced a revised edition of a book on the concept of immortality that he wrote thirty years earlier.[47] He begins by considering the relation between the mind and the body. He dismisses the view that this is a pseudo-problem. 'No doubt', he writes, 'by a careful arrangement of verbal symbols and by defining terms in very general ways, it is possible to avoid contradiction when speaking of mind and body as identical—but it is not possible to experience them as identical and the dualism of mind and body, thought and things, subjective and objective is a fact of experience'.[48] He then rejects materialism (by which he means the view that although the body affects the mind the mind does not affect the body) and 'parallelism' (according to which mental and physical events coincide without interacting). He therefore opts for the common sense view that mind and body are ontologically distinct entities that interact even though we do not understand their mode of interaction. He concludes that 'Plato was right in thinking that mind is a higher kind of existence than matter and body, and that there is no good reason for supposing that mind depends for its existence on the organism with which it is associated'.[49]

Matthews then turns to the grounds for belief in immortality. He does not dismiss psychical research, although he is sceptical whether any firm conclusions can be drawn from it. In any case the latter would not establish the Christian hope. 'The most which could be demonstrated by this type of evidence is the continued existence of some human persons for some period after death. That, indeed, would be a remarkable and valuable achievement, but it would not give us the full assurance which we crave—that we may live eternally with God.'[50] So far as the philosophical arguments for immortality are concerned he rejects Plato's argument from the so-called 'simplicity' of the soul, but he accepts Kant's two arguments according to which belief in God demands an eternal life in which justice will be vindicated and scope given for the achievement of moral perfection. But the final and decisive ground for belief in immortality is the resurrection of Christ. Although all men are potentially immortal by nature Christians become actually so through participation in the risen life of their Lord. Furthermore this eternal life is made available here and now through the Holy Spirit.

With regard to the condition of the life to come Matthews affirms that we must be agnostic. Although he finds universalism attractive he rejects it on the ground that it is contrary to the teaching of Jesus. Yet he also finds the idea of everlasting punishment intolerable. If any soul is finally separated from God it will, he maintains, cease to exist. He is inclined to believe in an intermediate state in which spiritual growth will be possible. Lastly he holds that, although the material particles of our present bodies will not be re-assembled, we shall possess 'spiritual' bodies. 'We are bodies and spirits; we are not fully ourselves apart from our bodies, and we could not, it would seem, remain distinct persons unless we had something which corresponded to our bodies. St. Paul had the idea of a "spiritual body", and though we cannot understand how such a body is formed, there is no inherent absurdity in the conception.'[51]

The second point on which I ought to touch is of a general kind. Matthews (as was inevitable for a philosopher of his generation) wrote against the background of Absolute Idealism, and he was especially interested in the thought of Hegel and Croce. He rejected the monistic basis of Idealism. Following Christian tradition he adhered (as I have shown) to belief in God as the Creator who transcends all creatures in being, wisdom and power. Yet at one point he was influenced by Idealism. He was always concerned with the relation between religion, philosophy and art as 'forms of the spirit'. Also he held to the end of his days that religion—and of course he meant ultimately the Christian religion—represents the synthesis of the other forms. By this he meant that although art and philosophy have their own, autonomous, modes of spiritual expression, they will be fulfilled in religion as the supreme, and redemptively final, revelation of the divine Spirit.

The best formulation of Matthews' thought here is contained in a paper to which I have already referred. 'The thesis which I am prepared to defend is as follows: It is not certain that the triadic structure of the dialectic is true; there may be, for example, other Forms, such as morality, which should be included; but admitting, for the sake of the argument, that the three Forms of the Spirit are Art, Religion and Philosophy, I should maintain that Religion, in its ideal development, could be conceived as including the other two far more easily than either of them could be conceived as including religion.'[52]

Matthews made several valuable contributions to the analysis of religion. His assessment of Schleiermacher and Otto is, in my view, wholly valid. I also think that if one is to define religion at all his definition is as good as any (at least so far as the so-called 'higher religions' are concerned). He is also surely right in affirming that religion expresses two basic needs: the need to unify the world and the need to possess an ultimate ground of values.

However, Matthews' primary concern was not with religion in general, but with the Christian religion in particular. Here he fully recognizes the uniqueness of Christianity. Basing his reflections on the New Testament he affirms the centrality of the Incarnation. The Christian religion consists, essentially and distinctively, not in Jesus' teaching and example, but in the fact that he was the Word incarnate. Furthermore, to be a Christian is not merely to believe in the Incarnation as a past event; it is also to share in the life of the risen Christ through the Holy Spirit. I shall examine these claims in the next chapter.

Matthews' views on 'revelation' are also significant. Here he reflects a widespread tendency in twentieth-century thought. As

John Baillie showed,[53] many theologians in the period between the two world wars came to regard revelation as consisting primarily, not in a body of propositions, but in the personal self-disclosure of God himself—a self-disclosure that occurs through many media but that reaches its culmination in Christ. Dogmas are, though indispensable, secondary. This view was propagated chiefly by Reformed theologians (in England notably by William Temple). From the Roman Catholic side it has recently been affirmed in the second Vatican Council's Constitution *De Divina Revelatione*.

Yet Matthews' main interest was not in the historical or even phenomenological study of religion but in natural theology. Here he made five basic points. First, God's existence cannot be proved by a logically coercive demonstration. Secondly, therefore, belief in him must rest ultimately on intuition or experience. Thirdly, in this it resembles other basic beliefs. Fourthly, however, it must satisfy rational criteria. We must be able to show that theism is the only, or at any rate the most satisfactory, hypothesis for a final understanding of the world. Lastly, intellectual inquiry in every sphere (not least in the natural sciences) is animated by an act of faith in the world's intelligibility.

All these points have parallels in the writings of other twentieth-century philosophers and theologians. Here are some examples.

(1) There has been an increasing recognition during this century that it is impossible to demonstrate God's existence with logical certainty from non-theistic premises that are accepted by believers and unbelievers equally. E. L. Mascall crystallizes this fact as follows. 'It has, for example, been maintained by some scholastics that the famous "Five Ways" by which St. Thomas Aquinas argues for the existence of God are pure exercises in syllogistic deduction; that the premises "if anything exists, God exists" and "Something does exist" logically imply the conclusion "Therefore God exists". Their difficulty is how to prove the truth of the major premise without already begging the conclusion, and I for one cannot see how this can be done.'[54]

(2) Hence Christian philosophers have been continually forced

to regard the data indicated in the premises of the theistic proofs, not as data from which the existence of God can be inferred, but as means by which it is directly intuited or apprehended. Hence Mascall continues thus. 'There is, however, another school of thought, of which, in spite of their differences on points of detail, Dr. A. M. Farrer, Dom Mark Pontifex and Dom Illtyd Trethowan are representative, according to which the function of the arguments is to direct the attention of the mind to certain features of finite beings which can easily be overlooked and from which the existence of God can be seen without a discursive process. There is no question of asserting that, in this movement, we have a direct and immediate apprehension of God; direct, if you like, but not immediate, for it is mediated by and in our apprehension of finite beings. For Pontifex and Trethowan, if we grasp the existence of finite beings as it truly is we shall see that it is simply identical with their relation to the transcendent cause which is their Creator; for Farrer, we shall similarly grasp what he calls the "cosmological idea", the idea of God-and-the-creature-in-relation. It is not denied that in making this approach there is a great deal to be done in the way of argument and discussion; but it would be held that the purpose of this argument and discussion is not to win assent to a logical demonstration, but to put the hearer in the frame of mind in which he will be able to apprehend finite beings as they really are, to get beyond both the superficial level of sensible phenomena and also beyond even the particular individual existence of the finite beings themselves, to the Creator upon whose incessant activity their very existence depends. What can thus be apprehended, it is alleged, is neither the-creature-without-God nor God-without-the-creature, but the-creature-deriving-being-from-God and God-as-the-creative-ground-of-the-creature: God-and-the-creature-in-the-cosmological-relation. To use another term, there is a *contuition* of God, the apprehension of the presence of the cause in a perceived effect."[55] To the names that Mascall cites one could add those of John Baillie, H. D. Lewis and John Hick who have also insisted, in their differing ways, that intuition or experience is required for the knowledge of God in all its forms.

(3) In this century many philosophical theologians have also pointed out that direct acquaintance with finite entities is the basis of judgments we make concerning them. A particularly clear parallel to the main example that Matthews gives is afforded by Kemp Smith in a lecture entitled *Is Divine Existence Credible?* Having stated that our knowledge of the divine is always mediated by the non-divine, he urges that this knowledge is 'identical in type' with our knowledge of other selves. Concerning the latter knowledge he writes: 'Now it may be agreed that we do not experience other selves—any more than we experience the self—in isolation from all else, and certainly not independently of their bodily actions; but while doing so, we may still maintain that through, and in connection with, these bodily activities other selves are experienced with the same immediacy with which we experience the self, our conviction as to their existence being based on directly experienced fellowship, and not upon inference.'[56]

(4) Yet even those who affirm that religious knowledge is intuitive also frequently stress that it must satisfy rational criteria—that it must cohere with and if possible explain the relevant data. Thus I. T. Ramsey, while insisting that faith is based on a 'disclosure' of reality, held that its claims must be tested in an appropriately metaphysical manner. 'A model in theology does not stand or fall with, a theological model is not judged for its success or failure by reference to, the possibility of verifiable deductions. It is rather judged by its stability over the widest possible range of phenomena, by its ability to incorporate the most diverse phenomena not inconsistently.'[57] A. M. Farrer put the point even more strongly by affirming that we cannot argue that finite entities *allow* of being read as creations of the Infinite without also arguing that they *demand* to be read as such.[58]

(5) On the fact that the metaphysician presupposes the intelligibility of being F. C. Copleston has recently written thus in answer to a hypothetical objection. 'If this is a presupposition, it is not made by the metaphysician alone. For instance, unless the imagined critic is prepared to maintain that the scientist sets out to

impose a purely subjective construction on an unknowable X, he must admit that the scientist "presupposes" the intelligibility of being. For if the opposite were presupposed, who would apply himself to scientific inquiry? To be sure, scientific hypotheses are constructions of the human mind. But they are constructed with a view to knowing the world better. Hence, if the intelligibility of being is presupposed in metaphysics, it is presupposed also in natural science. And if the presupposition is legitimate in natural science, it is legitimate also in metaphysics.'[59]

All five theses are well illustrated by the last chapter of A. C. Ewing's *The Fundamental Problems of Philosophy*.[60] I quote Ewing both on account of his eminence as a philosopher and because he and Matthews were almost exact contemporaries. Ewing holds that although we cannot prove God's existence with logical certainty 'it may be argued that according to the scientific principle that we should accept the hypothesis which brings the universe nearest to a coherent rational system theism should be accepted by us'.[61] On these grounds Ewing accepts the cosmological and teleological arguments. He further maintains that belief in God rests ultimately on an intuition or experience that is obtainable by all men (although it reaches its supreme degree of intensity among the mystics). Finally he claims that 'religious beliefs are after all only in the same position as other fundamental beliefs in not being strictly provable. By "fundamental belief" I mean a belief presupposed by a whole important department of human thought. When we consider belief in memory, in an external world, in minds other than one's own, in induction, in ethics, we are driven back to something which we either cannot prove at all or at least cannot prove in a way which wins general agreement among philosophers, yet we continue unflinchingly to hold the beliefs. It is doubtful whether it is possible to give a more plausible case for the reliability of induction or for the existence of the physical world than it is for the existence of God, only the ability to cognize God is less widely distributed or at least less widely developed than the ability to cognize the physical world and see the validity of inductive inferences.'[62]

I have merely attempted to show that although Matthews arrived at his theistic principles by independent reflection he has the support of many modern thinkers (of whom some would differ from him in other ways). Obviously I cannot here discuss the principles at the length they deserve. I can only say that I have attempted to amplify and defend them (though without enumerating them as such) in a book I wrote six years ago.[63] At the time of writing my knowledge of Matthews' work was, regrettably, small; so that I was not influenced by him. I am now encouraged by our agreement.

There are, however, two possible criticisms with which I must deal. Matthews' approach to theism was formed against the background of philosophical ideas that may now seem to be old-fashioned. In particular he gave little attention to the challenge of logical positivism. Yet a writer's views are not necessarily invalidated by the fact that he did not answer objections that were subsequently brought against them. In any case so far as the verification principle is concerned it is enough to observe that Matthews considered the 'God-hypothesis' to differ from scientific hypotheses in so far as it is verified, not by sensory observation, but by spiritual experience of a distinctively religious kind. I am sure that he would have effectively developed this crucial point of difference, and in general made a distinctive contribution to the debate engendered by *New Essays in Philosophical Theology*, if he had belonged to a later generation.

Secondly exception may be taken to Matthews' claim that the theistic proofs make theism 'highly probable'. The essence of the criticism is that because the theistic postulate is wholly unique we cannot probabilify it by empirical evidence (as we can probabilify a scientific hypothesis). Thus we cannot compare universes that we know are designed by a cosmic Mind with those that we know are not thus designed in order to conclude that our universe was 'very probably' thus designed. I think Matthews would have granted this point. In at least one of his writings he makes it clear that in saying that theism is the most probable hypothesis he means that it is the most reasonable one (i.e. the one that best fits all the data).[64]

I turn now to Matthews' account of the particular 'proofs'. I am sure that he is right in affirming that in so far as the Anselmic and Cartesian forms of the ontological argument involve a transition from thought to reality they are invalid. Much has recently been written on the argument. Yet I am still convinced that it is impossible to move by logical necessity from the idea of God as a 'most perfect' or 'necessary' being to the postulation of his existence. Thus in my view John Hick has shown that Malcolm's reformulation of the argument is vitiated by a failure to distinguish between ontological and logical necessity.[65]

I also agree with Matthews' claim that all knowledge involves the two ontological assumptions he describes. Yet these need to be sharply distinguished from the ontological argument. They do not carry any theistic implications of a logically invincible kind. Moreover I find myself unable to endorse Matthews' claim that 'if there is any truth there is absolute truth, and if there is absolute truth there is absolute reality'. I suggest that here he has been influenced by Idealistic tenets that he has insufficiently examined. Nevertheless I do not wish to press this opinion. There are very few points in Matthews' writings at which this influence can be detected. Also he based his rational theology on other arguments that I shall proceed to examine.

Matthews is surely right in giving primacy to the cosmological argument. The fundamental fact to be explained is the sheer existence of anything at all; and the only explanation lies in the hypothesis of a self-existent Creator to whom we can ascribe spiritual properties according to the *via eminentiae*. Obviously the argument is exposed to objections that must be answered (and that I have attempted to answer in the book to which I referred earlier in this chapter). Here I wish merely to urge that full account be taken of Matthews' view that causality cannot be reduced to Hume's 'constant conjunction' or even to Kant's subjectively imposed 'categories', but that (although we know it first through our own experience of mental and physical effort) it is an objective constituent of the external world. Matthews refers to Whitehead. A more recent defence of causal necessity has been cogently offered by Brand Blanshard.[66]

I fully sympathize with Matthews' desire to construct an argument for God's existence from the fact of morality; but I am compelled to query his mode of construction. I agree with him that moral ideals are objective in the sense that they are not merely expressions of our feelings and attitudes. I also agree that if we grant them objectivity in the sense of independent being we must locate them in God's mind. Yet need we grant this? Does objectivity in the first sense entail objectivity in the second? Why should not moral values be *merely* ideals that we envisage as norms and goals of conduct? To take a mathematical analogy that Matthews himself adopts, most of us do not posit a transcendent location for the idea ltriangle presupposed by geometers (although such a location was posited by Plato).

Rather I should say that the divine ground of moral values becomes apparent only when their obligatory character is taken into account. I agree with P. R. Baelz when he asserts that the world of value 'although in a sense an ideal world is also real by virtue of the pressure which it exercises upon us in moral experience'.[67] It is the fact of moral obligation that demands a theistic explanation; for it cannot (so I maintain) be satisfactorily explained except in terms of a divine lawgiver who (if his law is to have moral authority) must be absolutely good. At the same time I agree with Matthews' emphasis on all that is true in the concept of moral autonomy. The Word who commands us from without is also the Word who enlightens us within. Hence God calls us to obey his law by our own insight and by the exercise of our free will. Hence too he calls us to recognize his law as the law of our being—as the principle determining our self-fulfilment.

Nevertheless, I think that Matthews might have been prepared to concede the force of my criticism. He always stressed the reality of moral obligation. Also in at least two places he linked obligation to values in the way that I have urged is necessary. In his *Essays in Construction* he wrote that when a man 'attains the level of personal existence' he 'becomes aware of a realm or order of values or ideals and recognizes them as having a supreme right to be, and hence as having an overriding claim on his allegiance'.[68] On the next page he added that 'these values have an indefeasible claim on our service, and at the same time we are free to direct our actions in accordance with these values or to refrain from doing so'. Later, in his *The Purpose of God*, he affirmed, with reference to the evolution of mind, that 'the point at issue is whether mind when most completely self-conscious, that is, when most completely mind, does not recognize that there are values which possess absolute authority and does not regard itself as owing an unconditional obligation to them'.[69]

There can be no doubt that Matthews made a major contribution to the presentation of the teleological argument. Here he merits comparison with F. R. Tennant, G. F. Stout, and A. E. Taylor. I agree that efficient and final forms of causality do not exclude each other. Here too I think that Matthews' references to Leibniz deserve more attention by those who consider science and metaphysics to be incompatible. It also seems to me that Matthews has brought a strong objection against the view that nature's order can be explained through the random combination of finite particles. Finally he is surely right in maintaining that the ideas of 'natural selection' and 'emergent evolution' are teleologically insufficient. The former presupposes the existence of variations, or mutations, that are to be selected. The latter is descriptive, not explanatory.

Chiefly it seems to me clear that the most cogent form of the teleological argument is the one that Matthews stresses. If we admit an ontological distinctness between mind and matter, so that mind is not reducible to matter any more than matter is reducible to mind, we cannot explain the emergence of mind from matter unless we attribute it to a creative Mind, a personal God who to some extent transcends the universe. Furthermore, if we postulate a cosmic Designer for the emergence of mind we must also postulate him (as Stout observes) for the creation of mind's bodily antecedents.

The unique strength of the teleological argument in this form is as follows. Some forms of the argument depend on a calculation of probability. Matthews (rightly in my view) contended that the argument from probability is groundless; for it implicitly presupposes an element of stability that it explicitly denies. Moreover, it has often been argued that even if we admit that a probability-calculus is applicable in this sphere the improbability of a fortuitously ordered universe is so great as to be unacceptable. I endorse this view also. Yet an explanation of mind's emergence solely in terms of its physical matrix is, not merely improbable, but impossible. Again, some forms of the argument depend on an emergence of novelty within the material realm itself. Thus it has been said that organic matter involves changes that cannot be explained in terms of its inorganic base. Here also I agree; but I admit that the question is open to scientific dispute. In any case the difference between the inorganic and the organic is a difference *in pari materia* whereas the difference between all forms of matter and mental processes is an absolute difference of kind.

Scientific advance since Matthews' day does not in the least affect his thesis; for the latter is a metaphysical postulate that is required in order to explain all possible data that scientists discover and all possible theories they produce. Thus the most elaborate exposition of the D.N.A. 'coding-system' does not explain the development of a single embryo from a non-sentient mass to a human being. The more we know of mind's evolution from matter in every form and on every scale the greater its mystery becomes. As the scientific 'gaps' close the greater the metaphysical 'gap' becomes.

Whether the God whom we thus postulate is infinite and good is a further question (as Matthews acknowledged). My own view is that if we must trace back mind's advent to its material background we cannot consistently stop with the latter. We are irresistibly driven to the idea of a God who is, not merely a Platonic *Demiurge*, but the Maker of all that is. Also I think that Matthews gives reasons for affirming, in spite of evil, that the cosmic designer is good. Nevertheless (as he himself would admit) if belief in God's infinity and goodness can be established at all by rational arguments it can be so most effectively through the cosmological and moral arguments.

However, is mind distinct from matter? Can the premiss of Matthews' teleological argument be sustained? This brings me to his book on immortality. Matthews begins by affirming the distinctness of mind from matter, and so the possibility of entertaining the idea that mind can survive apart from its material conditions. It must be admitted that he did not substantiate this affirmation with the detail of which he was capable. In his defence I would only say that his failure to do so was occasioned, not by impercipience or laziness, but by his conviction that the 'dualist' hypothesis (the view that mind and body are distinct entities that interact, however mysteriously) is an immediate datum of experience. I agree. There are many forms (some more sophisticated than others) of materialism and behaviourism. Yet although they require an examination that Matthews did not give they all founder ultimately on a simple, irreducible, fact of self-consciousness. I know that I am a spiritual self simply in the act of knowing it—not, indeed, in quasi-mystical isolation, but through my experience of 'owning' my body by my willed acts and through my response to my environment.[70]

I shall not discuss Matthews' views on immortality because he propounded them in a designedly 'popularizing' work, and so did not elaborate them as he elaborated other topics. Nevertheless his remarks distil careful and prolonged reflection that again elicits my agreement. It seems to me that he shows the right balance between belief and agnosticism in an area in which the limits of human knowledge become apparent more quickly than in any other. I am especially impressed by his attempt to combine 'nature' with 'grace'. On the one hand he supplements his own form of the moral argument by invoking Kant's 'practical' reasons for postulating immortality. On the other hand he asserts that even if every soul is potentially immortal this potentiality is supernaturally actualized through participation in Christ as the incarnate and risen Son of God.

I therefore submit that Matthews made a valuable and distinctive contribution to the philosophy of religion and philosophical theology. The only point at which his reflections are 'dated' to any substantial extent is where he relates them to the Hegelian triad of Art, Religion, and Philosophy. Yet even here his thought is purely hypothetical. He says merely that if this dialectical structure is accepted religion can be plausibly regarded as its culminating stage. His own account of religion and its relation to philosophy owes scarcely anything to Hegelianism.

3
Christology and Ethics

In the first chapter I showed how Matthews maintained that Christianity consists, not in the imitation of a merely human Jesus or in acceptance of his merely human teaching, but in belief in him as the incarnate Word. This point is so important that I do not apologize for offering three more extended quotations in the chronological order of the works from which they are taken. The first is as follows:

> We should, however, be giving a very imperfect representation of the Christian view if we confined ourselves to the teaching of Jesus as the supreme example of Ethical Monotheism. It is true that for the New Testament no less than for historic Christianity the central point is the person of Jesus. Christianity is Christ rather than the teaching of Christ. There can be no doubt that Jesus made the most exalted claims for Himself as the supreme revealer of God, and that this claim was admitted by His followers and formed the basis of their religious life. This at least is clear even if we do not admit that He ever asserted Himself to be the Son of God in any unique sense or used the words, 'He that hath seen Me hath seen the Father'. Only an inconceivably perverse criticism could refuse to admit that in the earliest records of the Christian religion there is a belief about Christ which at least corresponds to and could form the germ of the Christian doctrine of Incarnation.[1]

Many years later Matthews wrote similarly:

> The Christian belief about God is governed not only by the teaching of Jesus, but by the belief of the Apostles that He was the supreme and final revelation of God. The Incarnation is at the centre of all Christian theology and must determine for it the idea of the divine nature. In its simplest form this belief is summed up by St. Paul, 'God was in Christ

reconciling the world to Himself'. There is little in the New Testament which could be described as philosophical speculation about the divine Being. The existence of God is taken for granted, and the character of God is that of the Father of the Lord Jesus Christ. The love of God is revealed in Christ who 'came down from heaven' for us. It seems that in the wonder of that saving act of God all doubts about the love of God were swallowed up. For those who had seen God 'in the face of Jesus Christ, the questions were answered, or rather were irrelevant.[2]

Still later he commented thus on Claude Montefiore's treatment of the gospels:

The whole aim and purpose of the Evangelists is to bear witness to a supreme and unique event, the act of God in the coming of Jesus the Messiah to fulfil the prophetic aspirations of the Hebrew religion. Of course, Montefiore did not believe that this was true and to that extent he was precluded from feeling an inner sympathy with the main theme of the Gospels, but I think that he does not sufficiently recognize the true character of the books which he is interpreting. He has given us much valuable information about the higher ethical teaching of the Rabbis and has helped us to take a juster view of the Pharisees. He has shown that the moral teaching of the Gospels was not so far from the standpoint of Jewish religion at its best as we had supposed. All this is admirable and useful, but if I may say so, it does not appear to go to the heart of the matter. The real question is not whether the ethical teaching of Jesus is original but whether He is the Son of God.[3]

Matthews admits that the doctrine of the Incarnation is not often explicitly affirmed in the New Testament. Yet, he maintains, the apostolic writers constantly describe Christ's revelatory and redemptive activity in terms that imply his Godhood. Thus he wrote that Christ 'is perhaps never explicitly spoken of by St Paul as God, but His relation with God is one of identity of function with respect to men. He is the Son, He is the Word of God, He is the image of God, He is the Spirit, He is the heavenly Priest who opens the way to God. All these and other images are various modes in which the earliest Christian experience strove to embody its common conviction that Christ is the supreme and final revelation of God, that God is fully known, and His grace received only through Jesus Christ.'4

Four further points must be noted concerning Matthews' views on the Incarnation.

First, the Incarnation perfects the religion of Judaism by correcting its increasingly one-sided emphasis on divine transcendence. 'The result of the Hebrew reflection upon the nature of God had a defect which led to grave practical results. In the effort to preserve the Holiness of God free from defilement or compromise, the transcendence and separateness of God were over-emphasized. In the fear of degrading the divine by supposing that "He is even such an one as ourselves", there lurks the danger of putting Him so "far above out of our sight" that He becomes an unknown God. It is precisely this danger and defect which are removed by the Christian affirmation of God in Christ. That the supreme and adequate self-revelation of God is a morally perfect human personality is the completion of Ethical Monotheism.'5

Secondly, the Incarnation gives final meaning to the Christian idea of atonement. Christ's death was not an act of satisfaction or penal substitution. Its atoning power consists in the fact that it was the supreme revelation of God's love. 'The person of Christ Jesus brings to the Apostolic community the assurance of the love of God, but only because that person is interpreted in terms of a supernatural and divine act. Jesus of Nazareth dying on the cross has no message of the love of God to give: Jesus the Son of God in His passion is the assurance that God so loved the world.'6

Thirdly, the Incarnation is a final and complete revelation of God. 'The orthodox doctrine of the Incarnation has taught that in the Person of Jesus we have "God with us", and that He is the final and sufficient Revelation of God. Here there is an absolute in time and space, in a life subject to change and growth. If we were compelled to conclude that finality and absoluteness are by their very nature incapable of appearing within temporal and spatial conditions, we should have to reject the Incarnation doctrine of historical Christianity. We might, perhaps, still give a high place in our veneration to Jesus, and might still speak of "incarnation", but we should be saying something quite different from what the Catholic Church has meant.'[7]

To those who find the idea of a single, unrepeatable and absolute revelation of God in history unacceptable Matthews replies that we all acknowledge absolutes in other spheres. Thus we assume that truth is absolute. To deny this is self-stultifying; for even the relativist is bound to hold that it is absolutely true that all truth is relative. Again some works of art (for example the music of Bach) can be called final and unsurpassable.[8]

Lastly, although Matthews placed the main emphasis on the apostolic and post-apostolic testimony to the Incarnation he does not ignore the historical Jesus whose life and teaching are recorded in the gospels. Matthews admits that we cannot have complete knowledge of Christ's mind, not merely because the records are insufficient, but also because Christ, as the Son of God, was bound to experience God in ways to which there is no parallel in the lives of ordinary men. Nevertheless, we can know something of his inner life; and this knowledge is essential. Here Matthews criticizes Bultmann who holds that historical criticism does not permit us to know anything of Jesus' spiritual experience, but that our ignorance does not matter because Jesus' 'significance for the world lies not in what he experienced but in what he willed, not in his thought, but in his work'. Matthews finds Bultmann's position self-contradictory. 'What a man wills is the best possible evidence of the nature of his personality and his experience, for the will is the self in action.'[9]

How much, then, can we know concerning Jesus' inner life? Matthews answers this question as follows:

> The salient features of Christ's experience of God are its unbroken and triumphant character. Jesus comes before us as one who is unshakably sure of God, so sure that the question whether God exists would have no meaning for Him. There is no word of His which hints at the possibility of doubt. This assurance of God is immediate. It rests upon a direct apprehension and not upon any train of reasoning or conscious appeal to authority. This obvious truth has naturally led to the description of Jesus as the supreme mystic, and, if by mysticism we mean

simply the direct apprehension of God by the soul, the title is just; but if something more definite than this is intended the case is less clear. Attempts have been made to show that there is a regular outline of development in the spiritual life of the true mystic and that it passes through three or four definite phases. Miss Evelyn Underhill, in her beautiful and impressive book the *Mystic Way*, has tried to discriminate these phases in the life of Christ. In the opinion of the present writer the thesis of the book can only be substantiated by a *tour de force*, though the author has taught us much by the way. The spiritual experience of Jesus does not fall into any scheme of this kind, and we may specially observe that there is nothing really analogous to those periods of depression and dereliction which form a part of the personal history of 'normal mystics'.[10]

A few pages further on Matthews notes that Jesus perfectly exemplified both Schleiermacher's 'feeling of absolute dependence' and the spirit of co-operation with God's will. 'Throughout the words of Christ there is the sense of a dependence which is unlimited. It is God who clothes the grass of the field. Just as the Hebrew poets saw in nature and human life the direct action of God, so Jesus traces all events and all the life of man to the Creative Will. The "little faith" of men is shown by their refusal to rely upon God for natural no less than spiritual needs. But this feeling of utter dependence does not exclude the thought of co-operation; the fellowship with God is a true fellowship of will, and the spiritual consciousness of Christ is certainly not independent of moral effort.'[11]

I turn now to two writings in which Matthews deals solely with Christology. The first is an essay contained in a symposium entitled *The Future of Christianity* that was first published in 1927. The second is a book entitled *The Problem of Christ in the Twentieth Century* that consists in the Maurice Lectures he gave in King's College, London in 1949.[12]

Matthews begins the first of these by affirming the traditional doctrine of the Incarnation and its basis in the New Testament. The apostolic writers present Christ as, on the one hand, 'a divine Being to be worshipped without idolatry' and, on the other hand, 'one quite definitely human, with the passions, feelings, limitations of human life.'[13] Yet Matthews is dissatisfied with patristic statements of the relation between Christ's deity and his humanity. His first reason is that 'the thought of the Greek world was defective in its view of personality and did not even possess a recognized term for the concept'.[14] Secondly the Chalcedonian Definition's affirmation of two natures in the one person of Christ is untenable. 'Given two entities, which are in their essence different, it is impossible to bring them together into a real unity.'[15] At the same time Matthews is unwilling to endorse Ritschl's Christological substitution of value-judgments for metaphysical statements. 'The absolute separation between value-judgments and judgments of existence cannot be maintained, nor can we be content to think of Jesus as the revealer of the highest kind of life, leaving on one side the question whether he is also the revealer of the nature of the ultimate reality of the universe.'[16]

Matthews' own view is that Jesus is the supreme expression of the Word who to some extent is revealed in all human persons. 'In Jesus the divine Logos shines through all the acts and thoughts of the empirical ego. We find in him a human life and character completely unified by unwavering obedience to the Father's will, and illuminated by an unclouded consciousness of the divine presence';[17] so that 'the empirical, historical personality of Jesus is the adequate incarnation in time and space of the eternal Word'.[18]

Matthews begins his Maurice Lectures by affirming that in Christology the theologian is confronted with a two-fold given—the historical Jesus and the experience of the apostolic Church. He further maintains that the validity of this experience cannot be justifiably accepted unless it is based on the gospels. 'To say that the doctrine of the Incarnation is true and at the same time that we know nothing for certain about the real Jesus of Nazareth is to bring together two contradictory propositions.'[19] More specifically, although Jesus could not have conceived his deity in terms of the Nicene Creed he could not have been wholly unaware of his unique relation to God. 'The ultimate ground of the doctrine of the Incarnation must be in the self-consciousness of Jesus.'[20]

In order to exhibit a continuity between Jesus' self-consciousness and the claims made later for him by the Church Matthews concentrates on Jesus' proclamation of the Kingdom. Jesus identified himself so closely with the Kingdom as to imply that 'he *is* the Kingdom, at least in the sense that without him it does not exist'.[21] Yet how can we know that Jesus' claims to embody 'the end' were true, and not the delusions of a religious fanatic? There are two grounds (which were also the grounds that most impressed the first disciples): the sinlessness of Jesus—his unbroken consciousness of and obedience to the Father—and the experience of the Resurrection which 'must be the starting-point of any doctrine of the Incarnation'.[22]

In chapter two Matthews maintains the following contrasting theses. On the one hand in order to secure apostolic belief in Christ's deity the Nicene Creed and the Chalcedonian Definition were inevitable:

> There are still those who, following Gibbon in one of his less admirable moments, deride the whole controversy and the decisions of the Councils as strife about words and a futile making of mysteries. That appears to me to be simply stupid. The Councils were grappling with a real problem and were defending a belief which was really vital to the Christian religion. It was necessary so to understand the God-man that he was not merely a man-God, nor the Incarnation merely an apotheosis. It was necessary to maintain that the Incarnate Christ was really man and really God—both our Lord and our brother. The definitions, whatever their defects, had the merit of negating speculations which would have compromised the essential faith.[23]

On the other hand patristic theology was defective in four respects. I have already mentioned three of these. First, the Fathers lacked an adequate concept of personality. Secondly, they describe God as a self-sufficient being. Thirdly, although the Fathers desired to preserve the unity of Christ's person they were prevented from doing so by their assertion that Christ possessed two natures and, therefore, two wills. Lastly the very word 'nature' is inapplicable. Here Matthews acknowledges his debt to Schleiermacher:

Schleiermacher criticizes the two-natures Christology of the orthodox tradition very much on the same grounds as I have suggested and it is interesting to notice that he too sees in the doctrine of the two wills the climax of the paradoxes which it involves. He has, however, a more far-reaching objection which is worthy of our attention. He contends that the very use of the word 'nature' to refer to divine being as well as human places the problem of the Incarnation in a false setting from the start, for this language suggests that the Incarnation means the coming together of two types of being which are included within the same order or category. The term 'nature' is properly used only of finite things. Thus it is legitimate to speak of 'human nature' in the sense of those qualities which constitute human beings, as distinct from other finite beings, but it is quite improper to speak of divine nature, as if there were a class of divine beings who shared common qualities. This objection goes very deep. If it can be sustained, it implies that the two-natures way of thinking cannot be the expression of the full meaning of the Incarnation—the coming of God into human life.[24]

Nevertheless, Matthews is dissatisfied with Schleiermacher's own Christology. 'The essential idea of Schleiermacher's doctrine can be stated in one sentence—in Jesus Christ the God-consciousness is absolutely powerful. The absolutely powerful God-consciousness *is* the Incarnation for, says Schleiermacher, to ascribe to Christ an absolutely powerful God-consciousness and to affirm the existence of God in him are exactly the same thing.'[25] To this Matthews objects that it fails to secure the absolute uniqueness of the Incarnation. 'It might seem to follow from this that there are degrees of incarnation and that Jesus stands, as it were, at the apex of a series of imperfect incarnations. If the God-consciousness is the presence of God, then, one might suppose, wherever that is found God is, in some measure, incarnate. I think that Schleiermacher ought logically to have drawn this conclusion, but in fact he did not.'[26]

In chapters three and four Matthews states his own views. He proposes to examine the Incarnation in the light of modern psychology, and in particular the theory of 'the unconscious'. This theory raises various questions for Christology. The main one concerns the Libido (which Matthews defines as a 'subterranean stream which is, in a general and vague sense, sexual and from which is derived the motive force of the personality').[27] Was the Libido present in Christ? Matthews sums up his own view thus. 'If it is agreed that the possession of desires, impulses and instinctive drives is not in itself the consequence, or any part of, original sin, then we can hold both that the libido was in the personality of Jesus and that he was free from original sin. We should then have to hold that the Incarnate Lord was exempt from any perversion, enfeeblement or obscuration of the will and reason which is the consequence of original sin in other men; or to approach the subject from another point of view, we might hold that to him was given the full measure of grace to deal with the solicitations of concupiscent nature. If, however, we think that the impulses and instinctive drives are connected with original sin, either as a consequence or as a continuation of the original guilt, then we should have to conclude, either that the libido was absent from the personality of Jesus, or that he was not free from original sin. Either conclusion seems to be full of difficulty—the first psychological and the second theological.'[28]

After noting the possibility that Jung's theory of the unconscious may help us to understand Christ as the 'inclusive representative' of a new humanity Matthews turns to the subject of psychical research. He assumes the existence of telepathy and takes it to signify that at the unconscious level 'there is a linking of selves of such a kind that thoughts, emotions, and even memories, may pass from one mind to another without conscious communication'.[29] He then suggests that telepathy, raised to the highest degree, may explain the belief that Christ bore the sins of the world—a belief that he refuses to interpret in terms of penal substitution. 'Does not some faint gleam of light dawn upon us when we reflect upon the hidden *rapport* between selves of which telepathy is one evidence? We could imagine a case where all the barriers of the self are down and all the thoughts, emotions and desires of all the world flow in—the muddy stream of all human mental life. It does not overwhelm the conscious self, which remains aloof and master of the inconceivable mass of presented material, but all the thoughts are present and are part of the total experience. The conscious self knows them all, not from the outside but from within, yet in so far as they are evil or foolish, repudiates them and overcomes them. Would not such an experience be bearing the sins of many and the victory over them?'[30] Yet Matthews ends the chapter by asserting that 'psychology cannot give the final answer to any of the fundamental questions'.[31]

In the last chapter Matthews examines the Christological possibilities inherent in the concepts of 'pattern' and 'inspiration'. After claiming that the modern mind finds the ideas of 'activity' and 'event' more congenial than the concept of 'substance' he proposes that we conceive human persons as 'moving patterns of behaviour events—that is, of events which have an inner side, desires, motives, choices'.[32] Similarly, 'from the standpoint of time we must think of the will of God as a perfectly coherent moving pattern of acts of will, and a pattern which is not yet completed'.[33] The Incarnation can then be regarded as an identity of patterns between the divine will and a human will. 'A personal life of which it could be said that it is of the same pattern as the temporal will of God would be the supreme revelation of God; it would be God manifest "in the flesh".'[34]

However, Matthews proceeds to make two important qualifications. First, the concept of 'moving patterns' does not exhaust the nature of human personality. There is in every human person an irreducible 'I' or *ego* that is the subject of all experiences. Secondly, the concept does not exhaust the meaning of the Incarnation. 'Even if we were satisfied that, in one instance, a personal life showed the pattern of the divine will, we should still have to ask why, in this case alone, the pattern was perfect. From the point of view of the Christian faith we have still to weave into our theory, if possible, the belief that the Incarnation is a gracious act of God and that the Son "came down from heaven"—from the eternal into time.'[35] Hence Matthews finds himself compelled to speak of the Incarnation in terms of the assumption of a human subject by the eternal Word. 'The Incarnation then would be the taking of a created subject by the divine Logos and the intimate union with it so that the human subject, while never ceasing to be human and created, was so intimately joined with the divine that they formed, in the sphere of history, one person. These words are perhaps meaningless and, at the best, they indicate in an abstract way the conjecture which we might venture to make in a matter which is beyond our grasp. We come to a more concrete and comprehensible question when we ask, how could this union of divine and human subjects manifest itself in the life-experience of the God-man?'[36]

Matthews suggests that the answer to this question lies in the idea of inspiration. Whereas prophets and saints were partially and fitfully inspired, Jesus was wholly and continuously inspired, by the Spirit. Yet the same qualification is required here also. 'In view of what has been said already of the need for a metaphysical basis for the doctrine it is perhaps hardly necessary to state that I am not maintaining that the whole meaning of the Incarnation is to be exhausted under the category of inspiration. We are dealing now, not with the ultimate and eternal ground and significance of the doctrine, but with the person of Christ as a phenomenon in the order of history, and there I maintain that the fact of inspiration is the safest guide we have.'[37]

Although Matthews was primarily a philosophical theologian he was always deeply concerned with moral matters. I have already shown the ways in which he related morality to religion. He was also interested in philosophical ethics for its own sake. Early in his life he wrote a preface to an edition of Bishop Butler's *Sermons* that is still used. He also wrote on practical ethics. Here I shall restrict myself to two topics that sufficiently illustrate his approach. These are war and eugenics.

Matthews consistently adopted a non-pacifist attitude. He maintained the following theses. On the one hand the law of non-resistance enjoined in the Sermon on the Mount is not applicable to nation-states. It is meant for life in the Kingdom of God. This Kingdom, though partially present among disciples here and now, cannot be embodied in any terrestrial society; it will not come finally until 'the end' when God will fulfil his purpose for mankind. Matthews epitomized this conviction thus in a sermon delivered at Cambridge. 'Though the Sermon on the Mount is of inestimable value as the ideal at which we should constantly aim in our personal lives, it cannot, as it stands, be taken as a literal directive for action in society. It is the law of the Kingdom which can be perfectly fulfilled only in the realised and perfected Kingdom of God.'[38] On the other hand although no secular society is identical with the Kingdom some societies do, and others do not, accord to individual persons the respect that is due to them as those who have been created and redeemed by God. When a nation that is based on this respect is threatened by a totalitarian régime it has a duty to oppose or deter the actual or potential aggressor by armed force. On these grounds Matthews justified his country's war against Nazism and his later opposition to unilateral disarmament. On the former he wrote thus in 1940.

Western civilization has never been Christian, if by that we mean a tolerable approximation to the ideals of Christ, but it has been deeply affected by three great social values—law, freedom, and truth. In a general way it is true, as we have remarked, that these conceptions have been inherited from Roman justice, Greek thought, and Christian faith; but in fact they have all been mediated through the Church, which in the Middle Ages was the custodian not only of the Gospel, but of law and of the rights of rational thinking. Probably the most distinctive feature of Western culture is its regard for human personality as such, for on this the possibility of human freedom depends. This respect again depends on the influence of the Christian view of life, for which every human being is created in the image of God and is one of those for whom the Son of God died. This Christian civilization, real though grievously imperfect, is confronted by an opposing will which denies all the Christian values, one which destroys law, both public and private; which forbids the impartial search for truth and repudiates the natural rights of human personality. This is the crux of the business. The war is to decide which line the human race shall follow in the future.[39]

Matthews wrote more than once on eugenics. He was concerned with the possibilities of over-population and a genetic deterioration of the human race. Yet while being acutely aware of the problem he refused to accept any solution that he considered to be incompatible with Christian morality. Although he regarded family-planning as desirable, and although he thought it wrong to procreate a child who will almost certainly inherit a grave physical defect, he held that abortion is permissible only when the mother's life is in danger. Also he rejected the proposal that the quality of our race should be improved by artificial insemination. His reasons were as follows. First, such insemination would undermine the structure of the family. Secondly, even if it began by free consent it could soon become compulsory. Thirdly, there is no evidence that moral virtues are inherited. Lastly Christians believe that the 'end' of man is the supernatural transformation of character by the Holy Spirit.[40]

Matthews' defence of a 'just war' and his rejection of eugenic planning stemmed from two convictions. The first is one that I have already stated—namely, that the Kingdom of God cannot be equated with any terrestrial society. Thus in a lecture entitled *Biblical Principles and Social Progress*, having noted that 'the writers of the New Testament as a whole have no interest in the problems of contemporary social and political life', he affirmed that in the teaching of Jesus the Kingdom has three characteristics. It is 'the gift of God'; it is only partly present in history—and then only among believers; and its final advent is 'neither the result of an historical process nor is itself an historical event', but is 'the end of history, and has its existence in a new order of things—a new heaven and a new earth'.[41]

The second conviction is that men are, socially as well as individually, scarred by a sinfulness from which only Christ can deliver them. Here the most incisive passage occurs in a booklet that Matthews published in 1942.

> Against Utopianism Christianity sets its realistic view of human nature. Man is not a baffled and soiled angel, nor is he an innocent and undeveloped child. He is a being whose impulses are perverted, selfish and sensual. His reason and conscience often fight a losing battle against the forces of his disordered nature. I say that this is a realistic view

deterioration of the human race. Yet while being acutely awa[re of] the problem he refused to accept any solution that he considere[d to] be incompatible with Christian morality. Although he regard[ed] family-planning as desirable, and although he thought it wrong [to] procreate a child who will almost certainly inherit a grave physica[l] defect, he held that abortion is permissible only when the mother's life is in danger. Also he rejected the proposal that the quality of our race should be improved by artificial insemination. His reasons were as follows. First, such insemination would undermine the structure of the family. Secondly, even if it began by free consent it could soon become compulsory. Thirdly, there is no evidence that moral virtues are inherited. Lastly Christians believe that the 'end' of man is the supernatural transformation of character by the Holy Spirit.[40]

Matthews' defence of a 'just war' and his rejection of eugenic planning stemmed from two convictions. The first is one that I have already stated—namely, that the Kingdom of God cannot be equated with any terrestrial society. Thus in a lecture entitled *Biblical Principles and Social Progress*, having noted that 'the writers of the New Testament as a whole have no interest in the problems of contemporary social and political life', he affirmed that in the teaching of Jesus the Kingdom has three characteristics. It is 'the gift of God'; it is only partly present in history—and then only among believers; and its final advent is 'neither the result of an historical process nor is itself an historical event', but is 'the end of history, and has its existence in a new order of things—a new heaven and a new earth'.[41]

The second conviction is that men are, socially as well as individually, scarred by a sinfulness from which only Christ can deliver them. Here the most incisive passage occurs in a booklet that Matthews published in 1942.

> Against Utopianism Christianity sets its realistic view of human nature. Man is not a baffled and soiled angel, nor is he an innocent and undeveloped child. He is a being whose impulses are perverted, selfish and sensual. His reason and conscience often fight a losing battle against the forces of his disordered nature. I say that this is a realistic view

compared with that of the believer in Utopia, for it has the support of all history and experience. The man who thinks that the devil can be cast out by better education and by changes of the environment has never looked deeply into the strange soul of man; nay, he can never have seen clearly what is in himself.[42]

Matthews' Christology is wholly orthodox. It is based on two axioms. First, Christ was not a merely human figure; he was God incarnate. Secondly, the Incarnation must be understood in terms of the contrast between all creatures and their Creator. No man is divine. Yet in Christ, and in him alone, God, in the person of his Son, took a human life into union with his own.

At both these points Matthews stands in contrast with influential trends in twentieth-century thought. Many theologians have attempted to describe Jesus in purely human terms. Certainly some of them have also claimed supremacy for him. He is the only one, they have variously said, who was wholly obedient to God, wholly loving in his conduct towards his fellow-men, wholly possessed by the Spirit. Yet even so he was no more than *primus inter pares*; he differed from other men (from, say, Isaiah or St Francis) in degree, not in kind; he was relatively, not absolutely, unique.

Sometimes theologians have interpreted Christ thus against the background of the Jewish contrast between the Creator and his creatures. Yet they have also often done so because they have adopted a different account of God's relation to the world. If one starts from the Hegelian view that the whole world, as the Absolute's self-development, is divine one is bound to hold that Christ can exhibit divinity only to the highest degree.[43] Similarly if one follows Whitehead and Hartshorne in their belief that God and the world are interrelated in a process of mutual creativity one is obliged to hold that Christ can be no more than the supreme instance of this interrelation.[44]

Admittedly Matthews did not examine the scriptural grounds for the doctrine of the Incarnation with the thoroughness that would be required of a New Testament scholar (which he was not). Yet I believe he says enough, and that his affirmations are amply confirmed by recent trends in New Testament criticism. Although there are few passages in which Acts, the epistles and the fourth gospel explicitly affirm belief in Christ's deity they affirm it implicitly or indirectly in several ways—in (to take four examples) their description of him as 'Lord', their attribution of a creative function to him, their equation of his saving love and power with the love and power of God, and their claim that he embodied the life of the age to come. In all these ways the apostolic writers imply an identity of function and so, by implication, an identity of being between Jesus and God.

It also seems to me that Matthews was clearly right in further holding that it is self-contradictory to affirm on the one hand that Jesus was God incarnate and on the other hand that we know nothing certain concerning his earthly life. He also pointed out a fatal inconsistency in Bultmann's severance of Jesus' 'work' from his 'will'. Furthermore I think that the evidence entitles us to say that Jesus uniquely expressed the two modes of religious experience that Matthews describes. More specifically I am sure Matthews is right in maintaining that although Jesus was not explicitly aware of his divine status he must have been aware of standing in a unique relation to God. Finally I agree that a particularly clear sign of this awareness is the manner in which he associated the Kingdom's advent with his person and work.

On all the points I have mentioned in the preceding paragraph Matthews' judgments are supported by the writings of subsequent theologians who have become progressively dissatisfied with Bultmann's dichotomy between the Jesus of history and the Christ of faith. Here are some examples.

First, on the general necessity of grounding the kerygma in the words and works of Jesus himself Alan Richardson wrote as follows:

> The gospels provide abundant evidence that the Church in the apostolic and sub-apostolic periods did not preach Christ as a faceless eschatological event: it was important that believers should know how the risen Lord had come to be crucified, how he had lived and what he had taught. It mattered that catechumens should understand how he

dealt with people—with fishermen called to discipleship, with blind men and cripples and sorrowing parents, with grasping publicans and religious bigots, with the demon-possessed and with penitents or little children: if mattered because he was the risen One, who had left an example to be followed by the community of which he was the living Head. The moral appeal of the Jesus of history remains still a strong and converting factor in bringing men to confess him as Lord and Saviour, precisely because he is the Jesus *of history*, not the legendary hero of a morality play.[45]

Richardson's verdict co-incides with the so-called 'New Quest' for the historical Jesus among Continental scholars. This is summed up by R. H. Fuller's statement that 'despite Bultmann's brave attempt to prove that for the kerygma only the bare facticity (the *Dass*) of Jesus matters, the trend on all sides is to a recognition that the character and content of his history are equally important.'[46] More explicitly W. Pannenberg has affirmed that 'Christology is concerned, not only with *unfolding* the Christian community's confession of Christ, but above all with *grounding* it in the activity and fate of Jesus in the past'.[47] On the Christological importance of Jesus' teaching on the Kingdom as good an illustration as any is provided by some comments made by D. E. Nineham. He observes that the questions and difficulties that scholars have raised concerning the titles (such as Messiah, Son of Man and Son of God) ascribed to Jesus in the gospels are relatively unimportant. 'What is important is that our Lord did undoubtedly proclaim that in and with his ministry the Kingdom of God had arrived. And, of course, that declaration clearly raises questions about our Lord himself.'[48]

I shall now concentrate on Matthews' Maurice Lectures. His appeal to psychology shows his determination to interpret Christianity in the light of all the knowledge available. In my opinion the particular suggestions that he makes vary in their nature and plausibility. The categories of 'pattern' and 'inspiration' are obviously fruitful ways of describing the relation between the human Jesus and God. I also think that the question of the Libido in relation to Christ's humanity is a valid one. It is usually ignored by those contemporary theologians who are, rightly, not afraid to raise the most radical questions concerning the extent to which Christ's humanity resembled or differed from ours. I also think that Matthews fairly presents the solutions that are possible; but at the moment I do not feel able to decide between them.

I am less convinced by Matthews' appeal to the 'racial unconscious'. This idea is still only an hypothesis that, moreover, requires more clarification than Matthews gives. I agree that we cannot explain the New Testament's claims for Christ's universality by an appeal to the Platonic theory of universals that was presupposed by many of the Fathers. But I think that a metaphysical explanation in terms of the hypostatic union is required. The human Jesus is fully individual *per se*, even in his exalted state; he does not possess the ubiquity of God himself (as Lutheran theologians have maintained in their interpretation of *communicatio idiomatum*). Yet through his union with the Word Jesus possesses a universal efficacy or power. Also I am not convinced that telepathy helps us to understand Christ's 'sin-bearing'. I maintain that if Jesus incarnated God's holy love, and if he thereby possessed the universal power that I have indicated, we can understand his 'sin-bearing' in terms of his conscious mind without recourse to the concept of telepathy—a concept that is still obscure and for which there is still little solid evidence. Also Matthews himself says that it was Jesus' 'conscious self' that simultaneously repudiated and overcame the evil that crucified him.

However, I chiefly wish to note, not this or that merit or defect in this or that idea propounded in these lectures, but three characteristics of the author's approach. All these are supremely important for Christology. All too are separable from the psychological theories that Matthews tentatively offers. First, he affirms that patristic formulae were necessary in order to affirm belief in Christ's deity. Secondly, although he criticizes the Chalcedonian Definition he rejects any alternative that fails to conserve this belief. Hence he thinks it insufficient to say, with Schleiermacher, that Christ fully actualized the God-consciousness that is latent in all men. Thirdly, he admits that although psychology can help us to understand the effects of the Incarnation it cannot state its ground. Thus he says (in words I have already quoted) that the category of 'inspiration' applies, not 'to the ultimate and eternal ground and significance' of the Incarnation, but to 'the person of Christ as a phenomenon in the order of history'.

Matthews' qualifications are (to repeat) of the greatest Christological importance. Many modern theologians have criticized patristic theology on one or more of the grounds that Matthews states. Yet they have often added to their criticisms a total rejection of it. Secondly many modern theologians have failed to see that their own substitutes for the language employed by the Nicene Creed and the Chalcedonian Definition do not express the absolute uniqueness of the Incarnation. Thirdly this failure has sometimes been constituted by a further failure to distinguish between the ontological ground of the Incarnation and its psychological effects. This double failure, I hold, mars D. M. Baillie's *God Was In Christ* —a work that I admire in many ways and that is certainly one of the few outstanding books on Christology that have been written in English since the Second World War.

There are, however, points at which I find Matthews' Christology inadequate. First, his earlier account, in *The Future of Christianity*, of Christ as the supreme expression of the Word who is present in all men could be taken (as the Logos-Christology of the Apologists can be taken) to mean that Christ was a creature who differed spiritually from other men merely in degree. However, I do not wish to dwell on this criticism because this essay represents a comparatively undeveloped phase of Matthews' thought. Instead I shall examine his four objections to patristic theology. These have often been urged, and they have determined the shape of much modern Christology. Hence a consideration of them is crucial. I have already examined the one relating to God's self-sufficiency. I shall therefore confine myself to the others. I suggest that although they have substance, so that Matthews' adherence to them is intelligible, they are finally untenable.

(1) Matthews claims that the Fathers lacked an adequate concept of personality. Here we must distinguish between the word

and the idea. The Fathers may have lacked the word (*Prosopon* in the Chalcedonian Definition had a metaphysical, not a psychological, sense, as Matthews recognized). Yet they did not lack the idea. If those who framed the Definition had been asked they would have said that Christ's human nature included everything that we mean by 'personality', and that this inclusion was indicated by their assertions that Christ possessed a 'rational soul' and was 'consubstantial' with us. Furthermore we must remember that they took for granted the Biblical portrait of God as one who is personal in both his being and his acts. Here (as elsewhere) it is important to see the creeds in the context of worship—the *lex credendi* in the light of the *lex orandi*.

(2) Matthews claims that the Fathers failed to secure the unity of Christ's person. Yet Cyril affirmed that Christ's two natures become one in the person (*hypostasis*) of the Word as the second member of the Trinity. This was his great achievement in his controversy with Nestorius who, though affirming that Godhood and manhood co-existed in one person (*prosopon*), failed to show the ground of co-existence. Admittedly the Chalcedonian Definition's affirmation that the two natures concur in one *prosopon* or *hypostasis* could be taken as an endorsement of Nestorianism. All it explicitly asserts is that *somehow* the natures are inseparably one. But the Chalcedonian fathers certainly intended to imply that the source of Christ's unity as a single *hypostasis* lay in the Word's status as a divine *hypostasis* within the Trinity.[49]

It is, I think, possible that Matthews found this objection insuperable because he was looking for a psychological, not an ontological, unity. Two facts suggest this. First Schleiermacher criticized the concept of 'two natures' on the ground that they cannot coincide in 'an Ego which is the same in all the consecutive moments of its existence'.[50] Secondly, in his earlier essay on Christology Matthews, while recognizing that in the Chalcedonian Definition *prosopon* is not equivalent to our 'personality', objects that to postulate a union of two natures results in a figure who was not a 'unitary personality', and that it is removed from 'any possible psychology'.[51]

CHRISTOLOGY AND ETHICS

It is, of course, absurd to speak of two natures and two wills concurring in one person if by person we mean (in a psychological sense) 'personality'. But it is not necessarily absurd if we mean by 'person' (in an ontological sense) the divine *hypostasis* of the Word. Admittedly the hypostatic union (as the Fathers continually said) is a mystery that no finite mind can comprehend. Yet we cannot avoid mystery in any statement of the Incarnation. Furthermore, we cannot avoid positing two wills in Christ. If he did not possess a divine will he was not *God* incarnate; but if he did not possess a human will he was not God *incarnate*.

(3) I agree with Matthews that the application of 'nature' to God can be taken to imply that there is a class of divine beings who share common qualities. Yet philosophers and theologians have constantly applied the term to God in both Christological and non-Christological contexts. Two further points must be noted. First, all terms, when applied to God, require qualification. Secondly all positive descriptions of God imply an 'analogy of being' (*analogia entis*) between God and man. This analogy in turn implies at every point both a likeness and an unlikeness between the Creator and his creatures.[52]

I have dwelt on Matthews' objections to patristic theology for several reasons. They are obviously important in view of the position that the creeds of the early Church have continuously occupied in faith and worship; they have (as I observed) constantly influenced modern Christology; and, not least, Matthews himself felt them keenly. In order to place him here more precisely in his historical context I shall compare and contrast him with William Temple (whose views on the matter also have independent significance).

In an early contribution to a symposium entitled *Foundations* Temple wrote that the Chalcedonian Definition represented 'the bankruptcy of Greek patristic theology'. These words have often been quoted as if they constituted his final opinion on the subject. Yet later in his *Christus Veritas* he made the following admission. 'It is really not the formula, but the history of the whole controversy, that leaves the impression of bankruptcy. The formula did exactly what an authoritative formula ought to do: it stated the fact.'[53] On the next page he even by implication retracts his remarks on 'the impression of bankruptcy'. 'The formulae of the Councils', he writes, 'gather up and focus great movements of living thought, and are only really understood when related to those movements. Moreover, the successive affirmations do not represent discoveries but a progressive articulation of what was known all along.' He proceeds to affirm that the Incarnation can be finally understood only as a movement 'from above' whereby Godhood and manhood are united in the person of the Word; that this union is necessarily incomprehensible; and that the attempt to 'explain' it by recourse to the idea of a divine *Kenosis* is absurd.

Matthews stands in between these two views expressed by Temple. On the one hand he never passed such an adverse verdict on patristic Christology as Temple did in *Foundations*. On the other hand he never quite reached the full and unconditional acceptance of it that Temple expressed in *Christus Veritas*. On the one hand he recognized that Nicene and Chalcedonian terminology was required in the fourth and fifth centuries in order to affirm belief in the Incarnation. On the other hand he continued to doubt whether this terminology was still necessary or even whether it was meaningful. For the reasons I have given I do not think his doubts were well-founded although they were understandable.

However, I wish to emphasize, not these doubts, but Matthews' insistence, in spite of them, that the doctrine of the Incarnation requires a metaphysical foundation. Hence he regarded Ritschl's 'value-judgments' as christologically inadequate. Hence too he admitted that his own psychological terminology could not state the ontological ground of the Incarnation even if it could help us to understand its historical effects. And so he stands on the side of the creeds in affirming not only the fact of the Incarnation but also the necessity of stating it in terms of a unique union of being between God and man. By comparison with the importance of these affirmations his failure to clarify the mode of union is secondary.[54]

CHRISTOLOGY AND ETHICS

Matthews did not write extensively on the work, as he wrote on the person, of Christ. Nevertheless he repeatedly expressed his three-fold belief that Christianity is a gospel of redemption from sin; that this redemption occurs in the first place through our response to the forgiving love of God incarnate; and that it leads to participation in the life of the risen Christ. I have already quoted passages that illustrate this. Here are some more taken from Matthews' sermons.

'Conviction of sin', Matthews affirmed, 'has always been a primary element in Christian experience and Christian preaching, and it must always be so.'[55] This conviction is engendered by the vision of the Cross. Having admitted that it is possible to see in the Cross merely the tragic end of a holy man Matthews continues:

> But, if we are Christian believers, we cannot rest on this historical level. We pass on to the level of faith and its insight, and we see in the Passion far more than the deplorable and pathetic death of a hero. We see the sacrifice of the Son of God manifesting the divine judgement on sin, and the eternal love which forgives the repentant sinner offering him reconciliation and eternal life.
>
> In J. S. Bach's St Matthew Passion there is a moment which touches the quick of Christian devotion. It occurs after the chorus 'Lord is it I?' which is followed by the chorale 'My sin it was which bound thee, which did with woes surround thee, and nailed thee to the tree'. That is the deepest answer to the question, Whose fault? The Saviour came to be a sacrifice for the sin of the whole world, for all men and to redeem them—including me.
>
> This personal and individual relation with the Saviour is inescapable in the New Testament and in Christian experience ever since. 'He loved me and gave himself up for me', says St. Paul, and we can hear the wonder and the gratitude in those simple words. They are at the heart of the gospel.[56]

Furthermore, Christians are called to share, through the Spirit, in the life of the crucified and risen Christ. On this an especially telling passage occurs in a sermon entitled 'Life through Death':

> The Christian belief in the Resurrection is a gospel. It is not a belief

that some anonymous individual has risen but that the Son of Man has overcome death and dies no more.

It is the belief that the love which led Him to die for man's redemption and seemed to be finally frustrated and defeated on the cross was really triumphant and that the Man who claimed to be, in a unique sense, the Son of God truly revealed the divine nature as love and, therefrom, that, in spite of every disconcerting appearance to the contrary, the ultimate meaning of the universe is not blind chance, or destiny, or impersonal reign of law, but the love of the Father.

This indeed is good news, but how does it become a word of salvation for me?

To answer this question we can turn to the books of the New Testament which show us the gospel of the Resurrection in action. We are risen with Christ says St. Paul, and the thought echoes through all the Christian centuries.

The Resurrection is not a work of wonder and power done apart from us at which we may marvel but in which we cannot share. By faith we may be incorporated into Christ and be partakers of His sacrifice and His victory. The experience of the Son of Man dying and rising again in new and nobler life is the pattern for our personal development.[57]

Matthews stated the essence of the New Testament's teaching on the Atonement. Paul and John believed in Christ as their Redeemer not merely because he was a perfect man who inspired them by his example but because he incarnated God's love and imparted to them the power by which he conquered evil on their behalf. Admittedly some Christians will wish to supplement Matthews' account by invoking other concepts (such as those of 'satisfaction' and 'penal substitution'). Yet even if these are valid—and my own view is that they are invalid in the rigid form in which they have often been presented—they are insufficient. Let us suppose that Christ's death was an act whereby God's justice was satisfied and sin's penalty paid. This act would still not save us unless we responded to the divine love that is its ground. Similarly the Resurrection does not confer eternal life even on those who believe in its eschatological significance unless they receive the life of the risen Christ himself.

One further, general, point is worth noting. The saving work of Christ has been interpreted in two main ways. According to the first way Christ saves us by communicating to us the divine life that he once lived on earth. This interpretation is typified by the claim made by many of the Fathers that God became what we are in order that we might become what he is. According to the second interpretation (typical of Protestantism) Christ saves us by the sacrificial quality of his death. These interpretations have often been falsely opposed to each other. Matthews says enough to show that in his view both are required for preserving the fulness of belief in Christ as the Saviour of the world.

I do not propose to dwell on Matthews' ethics. As I have said, he was primarily a philosophical and doctrinal theologian. Hence it is as such that he chiefly deserves to be remembered. I merely wish to note two elements in his approach to moral matters. First, his rejection of pacifism and utopianism was due, not to a search for ignoble compromise or temperamental pessimism, but to his grasp of the New Testament's teaching on human sinfulness and the Kingdom's 'other-worldly' dimension. Secondly (and correspondingly) his ethical judgments were governed by the following question. What course of action is required by the status of persons as children of God who are members both of the *civitas terrena* and (potentially if not actually) the *civitas Dei*? This surely is the ultimate question that all Christian moralists ought to ask. And even if we disagree with the answers Matthews gives we can still profit by attention to his arguments.

4
Conclusion

The previous chapters, I hope, have sufficiently shown the quality of Matthews' writings. On all the main topics I have examined he made substantial and distinctive contributions that still merit the attention of philosophical and doctrinal theologians. Admittedly after his *God in Christian Thought and Experience* he did not write another work of comparable scope. This was due chiefly to the duties involved in his ecclesiastical offices, but partly to the fact that (to his disappointment) he was not invited to deliver the Gifford Lectures. Yet the totality of his writings earn him a place alongside C. J. Webb, William Temple, F. R. Tennant, and John Baillie among the philosophical theologians of his period.[1]

Throughout his writings Matthews exhibited an unusual balance and comprehensiveness of mind. These qualities are best illustrated by the ways in which he included and, moreover, integrated the following elements: reason and experience, reason and revelation, the natural and the supernatural, the spirit of free inquiry and reverence for tradition.

With regard to the first of these contrasts Matthews' position was this. On the one hand we cannot prove God's existence with logical certainty. We have a right to believe in it only on the ground of intuition or experience. On the other hand we must be able to show that the belief is the only (or at least the most satisfactory) answer to the questions posed by metaphysical reflection on the existence and nature of the world. Similarly Matthews held that reason is necessary in order to test any claim (even the Biblical one) to have received a special revelation of God. Thus he sought to avoid both an excessive rationalism and sheer fideism. Matthews was also sensitive to both the natural and the supernatural dimensions of religious truth. His respect for the former emerges both in the emphasis on reason that I have just stated and in his insistence on the 'autonomy' of ethics. Equally he did justice to the supernatural character of Christianity by affirming his belief in the Incarnation and in the newness of the life that the risen Christ communicates.[2] Furthermore Matthews combined the spirit of free inquiry with reverence for tradition. This is especially evident in his Maurice Lectures. There although he seeks to interpret the person of Christ through psychological categories he admits that they cannot replace metaphysical ones. Correspondingly, although he criticizes patristic theology on many grounds he holds the conciliar creeds in high regard on account of the service they rendered in conserving belief in Christ's deity. Finally, he concludes by commending his views to the judgment of the Church.

Matthews' position with respect to all these contrasts is well illustrated by his response to his philosophical background. Although he was always intensely interested in philosophy both for its own sake and because of the light it sheds on religion he never allowed it to undermine experience and tradition or to take the place of supernatural revelation. Thus although Hegelianism was the dominant form of philosophy in his formative years, and although he was well versed in it, he repudiated its basic account of God's relation to the world as being contrary to the Christian concept of creation—a concept that he rightly considered to be essential to the Christian understanding, not only of God, but also of Jesus as God's incarnation. For the same reasons he rejected Whitehead's cosmology although he sympathized with Whitehead's view of God where it coincides with the teaching of the New Testament.

There are only two major points at which Matthews failed to effect a theological synthesis. First, he did not satisfactorily resolve the tension that he felt between two poles of Christian theism: the Biblical picture of a personal God who is involved in the destiny of mankind and later descriptions of God as self-sufficient Being.

6

Secondly, he did not finally reconcile ancient and modern categories of Christological thought. Yet his very failure exemplifies both his intellectual honesty and—the fact with which I am especially concerned here—his determination to include all facets of the truth as he saw it.

In his balance and comprehensiveness Matthews represented the best in the Anglican tradition that is associated with the ideal of a *via media*. Yet although this is true, and although it is impossible to think of him apart from the Church of England in which he held so many distinguished offices, it would be a mistake to conceive him within narrowly denominational limits. There is nothing selfconsciously Anglican in his writings; he showed an ecumenical spirit long before ecumenism became fashionable; and he could be critical of his own denomination.[3] Furthermore, he worked out his position in response to a philosophical more than a theological background. In short his type of intellect is, in the total context of Christendom, potentially universal even if it is one that is rarely actualized.

It is impossible to attach any finally adequate 'label' to Matthews. Apart from his Anglican background he had affinities with many schools of thought. Thus in his autobiography he says that in his early days he regarded himself as a 'Liberal Protestant' and 'Modernist'.[4] He continued to have much in common with those who are thus described. He always allowed due scope to Biblical criticism; he always opposed what he considered to be excessive claims to ecclesiastical authority;[5] and he was always anxious to take full account of secular knowledge in the presentation of religious beliefs. Yet he was free from the excesses to which Liberal Protestantism and Modernism are (or perhaps one should say were) prone. He never attenuated traditional Christianity in order to fall in with prevailing trends; he never thought that what is new is necessarily better than what is old;[6] and he fully realized that belief in God as an invisible reality runs counter to materialistic assumptions.[7] Above all he continually endorsed the Church's basic and distinctive doctrines of the Trinity and the Incarnation.[8]

My verdict is supported by the Times' obituary. Its author

observed that while Matthews 'insisted on claiming the name of modernist' he was 'in tone of mind much nearer the Cambridge Platonists' and that 'in all the fundamentals of the creed he was intensely orthodox'. Certainly he resembled the Cambridge (and indeed earlier) Platonists in several crucial respects—in his emphasis on intellectual intuition as the organ of religious knowledge, in his insistence on faith's intellectual requirements (on *fides* as *fides quaerens intellectum*), and in his irenical disposition that instinctively avoided denominational polemic. Yet he never confused the Gospel with Platonism (or indeed with any other philosophical system). Hence he was anxious to exonerate his predecessor at St Pauls, W. R. Inge, from the charge of sacrificing Christianity to Platonism. He spoke thus of Inge in a tribute paid on behalf of the British Academy. 'Though Inge made no secret of the fact that the philosophy of Plotinus was to him the most satisfactory of all metaphysical systems, he did not deserve the reproach, which was made by some, that he was more Platonist than Christian. In the Gifford Lectures he makes it plain that, like St Augustine, he did not find the Incarnation in Plotinus and that in this respect the Platonist was defective, nor did he fail to point out the inadequacy of Plotinus on the subject of sin and the difference between the "flight of the alone to the Alone" and the Christian hope of immortality in the Kingdom of God.'[9]

As I draw this book to a close I would stress that on all the main topics I have discussed Matthews' contribution is no less relevant today than it was when he wrote. Let us briefly reconsider them.

(1) There is the concept of God. Panentheism of an Hegelian type is no longer a major influence in the philosophical climate of the West today. Yet some theologians in this country and, even more, the United States are attracted to process thought. Admittedly the latter contains elements that can be assimilated to Christianity. However, there is a fundamental division between the view of God as the changeless Creator of all that is and the view of him as one who is constantly surpassing himself in response to an independently given world that creates him quite as much as he

creates it. The doctrine of creation is of ultimate importance historically, religiously and metaphysically. It is so historically because it distinguished Christianity from Stoicism, Neo-Platonism, and Gnosticism in the ancient world. It is so religiously because it is implied in the 'feeling of absolute dependence' that has always determined Judaeo-Christian faith. It is so metaphysically because it signifies one of the three or four basic ways in which God's relation to the world can be expressed. Matthews' adherence to it is all the more significant in view of his readiness to modify classical theism on the questions of God's self-sufficiency and impassibility.

(2) There is the importance that Matthews attached to reason in religion. Belief in God, he maintained, is supra-rational in so far as it rests on a spiritual intuition or experience that exceeds the limits of rational demonstration. Yet, he also maintained, it must satisfy rational criteria. In particular it must make the world ultimately intelligible by providing the most adequate answer to the questions raised by the cosmological, teleological, and moral arguments. A survey of the theological and religious scene today leaves me in no doubt concerning the relevance of Matthews' emphasis on the role that reason plays in the life of faith. Certainly Barth's rejection of natural theology has less influence than it had when Matthews wrote his major works. Yet one still has to reckon with the existentialist view (associated especially with Bultmann) that the Word of revelation is wholly self-authenticating. Also among British and American philosophers there is a tendency to substitute an analysis of religious language for the task of justifying theistic truth-claims by metaphysical argument. Moreover a new interest shown by many people in ecstatic experiences and in the spirituality of non-Christian religions has not always been matched by a concern for evaluating these experiences and judging between the conflicting statements that religions make concerning the nature of ultimate reality.

(3) The emphasis that Matthews placed on the doctrine of the Incarnation (and, consequently, on the doctrine of the Trinity) is no less pertinent today than it was thirty years ago. There are still

CONCLUSION

theologians who deny the first of these doctrines. In their view it is enough to say that Christ was a spiritually perfect man who fully revealed God's nature and will. This view is exposed to two objections that seem to me to be fatal. First it is not a reformulation of traditional Christianity but an abandonment of it. From the beginning Christianity was differentiated from both Judaism and Hellenism by its belief in Jesus as one in whom, and in whom alone, God had become man. And this belief has determined Christian spirituality in all its forms from one age to another. Secondly if Jesus was merely human it is impossible to justify the claims that Christians have continuously made for his uniqueness and finality; for it would then be possible to say that God's revelation in Jesus has been or will be equalled or even surpassed by his revelation in other men.

(4) Although Matthews was primarily a philosophical and doctrinal theologian, his ethical stress on the Kingdom's other-worldly aspect and on human sinfulness is still relevant. Few people (or at least few theologians) would now follow those Liberal Protestants of Matthews' youth who identified the Kingdom's advent with a divinely guided, and so inevitable, progress towards an ideal society on earth. Yet many Christians today are tempted to interpret their vocation chiefly, if not solely, in terms of support for humanitarian enterprises or even for political revolution. Matthews reminds us that although the Christian's plain duty is to rectify injustice and supply temporal needs as far as possible, no secular improvement is free from the possibility of corruption. Furthermore he reminds us that, in the words of the first Christian Platonist, 'here we have no continuing city, but we seek one to come'.

Matthews' thought was wholly objective in character. He expounded all the topics I have examined without basing his views to any degree on his own spiritual experiences. He rarely referred to the latter, and when he did so he was apt to be self-critical. Yet his writings constantly reflect his own faith in and love for God. Hence it is appropriate that I should close with a prayer that he wrote when he was Dean of Exeter. The prayer sums up the meaning of his life. Also it is one that all Christians can make their own.

Thou hast a work for me to do; O Lord, show it to me: Thou hast a place for me to fill; give me grace to fill it to Thy glory: Thou hast given me a soul to make; make Thou it for me, and build me into Thy spiritual temple, for Jesus' sake.

NOTES

PREFACE
1. *The Times*, 5 December 1973.
2. *Christian Meditations*, London 1974.

I. THE CONCEPT OF GOD
1. *God in Christian Thought and Experience* (G) (London 1930), pp. 60–1.
2. G. p. 104.   3. G. pp. 95–6.   4. G. p. 101.   5. G. p. 38.
6. G. pp. 173–4.   7. G. p. 162.   8. G. p. 163.   9. G. p. 80.
10. G. pp. 225–6.   11. G. p. 230.   12. G. p. 178.   13. G. p. 235.
14. G. p. 245.   15. G. pp. 241–2.   16. G. p. 243.
17. G. pp. 253–4. Cf. *God and Evolution* (London 1926), p. 36 where Matthews criticizes the evolutionary concepts of God advocated by Bergson and Alexander on the ground that 'they can never satisfy the deep desire of the spirit of man to stay itself upon One beyond change'. See also the first sermon in the anthology entitled *The Search For Perfection* (London 1957).
18. G. p. 254.   19. G. p. 255.   20. G. p. 256.   21. Ibid.
22. G. p. 248.   23. Ibid.   24. G. p. 26.   25. G. p. 203.
26. G. pp. 129–30.   27. G. p. 178.
28. *The Purpose of God* (P) (London 1937), p. 173.
29. P. p. 174.
30. *Studies in Christian Philosophy* (S) (London 1921), pp. 216–17.
31. G. p. 172.   32. G. p. 194.
33. *The Christian Faith: Essays in Explanation and Defence* (edited by Matthews, London 1944, pp. 57–8).
34. See his *Principles of Christian Theology* (London 1966), pp. 190–1.
35. Matthews explicitly stated his disagreement with Whitehead on this fundamental point. Thus he describes Whitehead's philosophy as 'a sophisticated Dualism'. (*The Religious Philosophy of Dean Mansel* (O.U.P. 1956), p. 22.) Similarly, in an unpublished paper he delivered to the London Society for the Study of Religion three years before his death, he affirmed that the idea of creation *ex nihilo* is an indispensable element in Christian theism and that he therefore found Whitehead's interpretation of creativity unacceptable.
36. Thus William Temple wrote that 'if God had no creatures to redeem, or if he had not redeemed them, he would not be what he is'. I take this quotation from A. M. Ramsey's *From Gore to Temple* (London 1960), p. 150. Ramsey

attributes this strain in Temple's thought to Hegelian influence. But no such influence is detectable in Matthews' denial of God's self-sufficiency.

37. *He Who Is* (London 1945), p. 107.

38. I have independently offered and sought to defend a similar interpretation in my *Concepts of Deity* (London 1971), pp. 23–5, 30–3.

2. RELIGION AND REASON

1. G. p. 7.   2. Ibid.   3. G. p. 9.   4. G. p. 10.   5. G. p. 19.
6. G. p. 20.   7. G. pp. 21–2.   8. G. pp. 23–4.   9. G. p. 67.
10. G. pp. 68–9.   11. G. pp. 93–4.   12. G. pp. 94–5.
13. *The Christian Faith*, p. 47.

14. Published in *The Modern Churchman* (December 1954), p. 279. Matthews was fully aware of the Freudian view that religious experience is a mere 'illusion' and that the idea of God is merely a psychological 'projection'. He makes the following replies. First, all ideas are psychological projections and many of them satisfy human needs, but we do not therefore regard them as necessarily devoid of objective reference. (*The Psychological Approach to Religion*, London 1925, pp. 20–1.) Secondly, 'the constant and almost universal appearance of religion wherever man has been found suggests that it is a response to some permanent aspect of the environment in which man exists'. Thirdly, 'the reality of religious advance, the whole process by which the human mind has passed from childish conceptions of the supernatural to sublime and elevating ideas such as those of Isaiah and Plato, is hard to reconcile with the theory that religion is pure illusion. For illusions are not fruitful; they tend to become more fantastic, and their consequences for life more depressing and disabling' (*Our Belief in God*, London 1936, pp. 28–9). Finally Freud begs the question by assuming that we know what reality is. He 'assumes that the world is known to be exactly as it was conceived by nineteenth-century materialism; and the religious consciousness is dismissed as the source of illusion because it finds Reality to be something quite different' (*Essays in Construction* (E), London 1933, p. 23).

15. London 1950, pp. 19–20.

16. Matthews proceeds to make two further points that are designed to harmonize reason with religion. First, reason has a synthetic as well as an analytic function (pp. 21–2). Secondly, rational processes of a synthetic kind are implicit in religion. 'There is no religious experience which does not imply some view of existence and of life, nor is there any religious experience which does not bring a new coherence and synthesis into the life of those who have it' (p. 23).

17. *The Idea of Revelation* (London 1923), p. 51. Matthews reiterated this view (with an accompanying stress on the authority of the Church in the realm of dogma) in an essay he contributed to a symposium that he also edited—*Dogma in History and Thought* (London 1929).

18. S. 80.   19. S. p. 120.
20. *The Christian Faith*, p. 50.   21. Op. cit., p. 51.
22. *Journal of the Transactions of the Victoria Institute*, Vol. LXXXIV, p. 120.
23. E. pp. 48–9.   24. S. pp. 166–7.   25. pp. 51–3.   26. S. p. 141.
27. S. p. 142.   28. S. p. 158.   29. S. p. 159.   30. p. 22.   31. p. 24.
32. p. 34.   33. p. 45.   34. p. 50.   35. p. 59.   36. p. 68.
37. pp. 71–2.   38. pp. 73–4.   39. p. 77.   40. p. 88.   41. p. 104.
42. Ibid.   43. p. 111.   44. p. 111.   45. p. 114.   46. p. 144–5.
47. *The Hope of Immortality*.   48. p. 12.   49. p. 15.
50. p. 22. Matthews made the same point in his Myers Memorial Lecture (*Proceedings of the Society for Psychical Research*, March 1940, p. 12).
51. p. 46.
52. *The Aim and Scope of the Philosophy of Religion*, p. 116.
53. *The Idea of Revelation in Recent Thought* (Oxford 1956).
54. *Words and Images* (London 1957), p. 84.
55. Op. cit., pp. 84–5.
56. Reprinted in the *Collected Papers of Norman Kemp Smith*, ed. by A. J. D. Porteous, (London 1967), pp. 391–3.
57. *Models and Mystery* (Oxford 1964), pp. 16–17.
58. *Faith and Speculation* (London 1967), p. 13.
59. *Religion and Philosophy* (London 1974), pp. 173–4.
60. London 1951.
61. p. 225.   62. p. 241.
63. *The Christian Knowledge of God* (London 1969).
64. In his essay entitled *The Idea of God* contributed to *An Outline of Modern Knowledge* (ed. by W. Rose, London 1931), pp. 56 and 63.
65. *The Many-Faced Argument* (London 1968), pp. 341–56.
66. *Reason and Analysis* (London 1962), chs. 10–12.
67. A lecture published in *Faith, Fact and Fantasy* (London 1964), p. 69.
68. p. 83.   69. p. 115.
70. For a recent and elaborate defence of dualism and interactionism (the view that mental and bodily processes are distinct but that they interact in inevitably unique ways) see H. D. Lewis's *The Elusive Mind* (London 1969).

3. CHRISTOLOGY AND ETHICS

1. S. pp. 53–4.
2. *The Christian Faith*, p. 46.
3. *Claude Montefiore: The Man and His Thought* (Southampton 1956), p. 14.
4. G. p. 71.   5. S. p. 54–5.   6. G. p. 81.   7. E. p. 92.
8. Op. cit., pp. 93–4.   9. G. p. 50.   10. G. pp. 50–1.   11. G. p. 53.
12. Published (Oxford) in 1950 (M).   13. p. 104.   14. p. 106.
15. p. 107.   16. p. 111.   17. p. 120.   18. p. 123.   19. p. 12.

20. Ibid.   21. p. 16.   22. p. 18.   23. p. 28.   24. p. 31.
25. pp. 32–3.   26. p. 33.   27. p. 45.   28. pp. 48–9.   29. p. 53.
30. pp. 54–5.   31. p. 60.   32. p. 67.   33. p. 70.   34. p. 71.
35. p. 73.   36. p. 80.   37. p. 82.

38. Printed in *The Cambridge Review*, 26 January 1952, p. 250.

39. *The Moral Issues of the War* (London 1940), pp. 31–2. Matthews stated his opposition to unilateral disarmament in a sermon preached in St Paul's on 16 October 1960. He held that nothing should be done that would weaken the West's defence against Communism.

40. See his Charles Gore Memorial lecture (1962) entitled 'Christian Humanism' and his Herbert Gray lecture published in *The Eugenics Review*, January 1962. Yet he did not regard human artificial insemination (A.I.D.) as being clearly wrong *per se* and in all circumstances. See his *Memory and Meanings* (pp. 348–52).

41. A lecture delivered at the Bible House, London (undated), p. 12.

42. *The Foundations of Peace* (London 1942), p. 14.

43. For a typical statement of Christology from an Hegelian standpoint see J. F. Bethune-Baker's *The Way of Modernism* (Cambridge 1927). A. M. Ramsey has shown that Gore's christological dispute with such modernists as Rashdall and Major rested ultimately on the fact that whereas he interpreted the Incarnation in terms of the Creator-creature contrast they interpreted it in terms of the Hegelian view that all men are, in varying degrees, expressions of the Absolute (op. cit., pp. 66–76).

44. For interpretations of Christ in terms of process thought see N. Pittenger's *The Word Incarnate* (London 1959), his *Christology Reconsidered* (London 1970), and D. A. Pailin's article entitled 'The Incarnation as a Continuing Reality' in *Religious Studies* (December 1970). Pailin gives full references to other writings.

45. *History Sacred and Profane* (London 1964), p. 240.

46. *The New Testament in Current Study* (London 1964), p. 147.

47. *Jesus—God and Man* (London 1968), p. 28.

48. *A New Way of Looking at the Gospels* (London 1962), p. 38.

49. Two facts make this plain. First, the Definition speaks of 'one and the same Christ, Son, Lord, only-begotten' and (yet more emphatically) 'one and the same Son and only begotten God'. Secondly the Council sanctioned Cyril's epistles in which the union of Christ's two natures is unambiguously grounded in the person (*hypostasis*) of the Word.

50. *The Christian Faith* (Edinburgh 1928), p. 393.

51. *The Future of Christianity*, p. 107. For various modern forms of the confusion between the metaphysical and psychological senses of 'person' in Christology see J. S. Lawton's *Conflict in Christology* (London 1947), pp. 251–70 and E. L. Mascall's *Christ, the Christian and the Church* (London 1967), pp. 23–47.

52. I also think that Matthews too readily dismissed the idea of substance.

Here I agree with Clement Webb's criticism in a review of Matthews' Maurice Lectures. Having maintained that the idea is christologically indispensable he observed that for Aristotle 'there was no opposition or inconsistency between *ousia* and *energeia*, substance and activity, as descriptions of reality' (*Journal of Theological Studies*, October 1951, p. 234).

53. London 1924, p. 134.

54. It was therefore right that R. V. Sellars should close his authoritative book on the Council of Chalcedon by quoting Matthews in support of his claim that the Council's Definition is permanently valid as an affirmation of the belief that 'Jesus Christ is the God-Man, in whom in his uniqueness Godhead and manhood are united' (*The Council of Chalcedon*, London 1953), p. 350.

55. *The Year Through Christian Eyes* (London 1970), pp. 85–6.

56. Op. cit., pp. 60–1.

57. *Christian Meditations* (pp. 53–4).

4. CONCLUSION

1. In a book entitled *Tendencies in British Theology* (London 1952), p. 81 J. K. Mozley linked Matthews with William Temple, C. C. J. Webb, and A. E. Taylor as the leading philosophers of religion in the period 1914–50.

2. The same combination occurs (as I have shown) in his approach to moral matters where he constantly recognizes the double status of Christians as those who belong both to 'this age' and to 'the age to come'. See also his sermon entitled 'Right Judgment' in which, having quoted the theological maxim that 'grace does not destroy nature but perfects it', he maintains that the Spirit's supernatural guidance and inspiration are always mediated by our natural faculties (*The Year Through Christian Eyes*, p. 96).

3. This is a point at which it is apposite to mention Matthews' views on the Thirty-Nine Articles of the Church of England. Throughout his life he was disturbed by the Calvinist portrait of God that the Articles present. In an expanded version (published in 1961) of a lecture delivered in Sion College, London he suggested three possible courses of action: the abolition of the Articles without their replacement, a revision of them, their substitution by a new statement of the Christian faith as understood by the Anglican church. Matthews advocated the third course and he suggested that the Archbishops' Commission on Doctrine might be revived to perform this task.

4. *Memories and Meanings*, p. 62.

5. Thus he affirmed that the earliest creed ('Jesus is Lord') should have remained the sole test for membership of the Church (M. p. 24). There is no contradiction between this view and the view (which Matthews also held) that conciliar creeds were necessary in order to amplify and defend belief in Christ's lordship.

6. See G. p. 111. Matthews urged that the religious symbols of the New

Testament are indispensable. (*The Year Through Christian Eyes*, p. 82-4). He concludes this sermon thus. 'The great symbols of our faith remain. Unless we use our imaginations they may be dark to us, as indeed will be all the world's poetry. Do we ever pray that our imagination may be enlightened? We have need to.'

7. In another sermon he wrote as follows. 'In our time the insight that the abiding and unchanging realities are invisible is particularly difficult to maintain because the whole emphasis of our civilization is on the world which we perceive and on the control of nature through discovery of its laws. The prevailing philosophy questions the assertion that there are realities inaccessible to our senses and, so far from agreeing that unseen and invisible things are the most real, would doubt whether they exist at all. Only by constant contemplation, in which we remind ourselves of our basic conviction that "God is spirit", shall we be able to stem the tide of current thought and feeling' (op. cit., pp. 100-1).

8. In an undated and (so far as I know) unpublished paper Matthews set down his views on the merits and defects of Liberal Protestantism. Its chief merit, he held, was that it encouraged an impartial study of the Bible through critical methods. But he insisted even more strongly that it was defective in three ways: it underestimated the importance of dogma, it tended to equate the Kingdom's advent with social progress, and it neglected the role that the New Testament assigns to the Church as the Body of Christ. Matthews makes it clear that two facts sharpened his awareness of these defects. First, on a visit to the United States he saw how radical Liberalism could degenerate into sheer humanism. On the second fact I shall quote his own words. 'Though there were many noble exceptions, it must be admitted that when the time came for the Church in Germany and elsewhere to face a deadly attack on its freedom to worship it was not, on the whole, Liberal Protestants who led the resistance. At that time of stress it was the men who held fast to the Confession of Faith, to the dogmatic system, who stood in the breach against the dictates of a tyrannical state.'

9. *The Proceedings of the British Academy*, Vol. XL, p. 269. Furthermore there was nothing in Matthews' outlook that gives justification for the view (held by some, though not of course all, Platonists) that philosophically gifted Christians constitute an elite who possess an insight denied to the mass of 'ordinary' believers. On the contrary he held that the theologian's task is to articulate the Catholic Faith as it is understood by the dogmas of the Church and so is accessible to all believers. He lamented the fact that theologians have not always understood the nature of their task. 'I cannot but think that too often theologians would have done better if they had constantly borne in mind that the beliefs which they analysed were the stay and inspiration of millions of simple persons who were trying to follow Christ by loving their neighbours and preserving their integrity against the lower standards of the world around them' (*The Year Through Christian Eyes*, pp. 90-1).

INDEX OF NAMES

Anselm, 5
Aquinas, St. Thomas, 7
Aristotle, 17, 28

Baelz, P. R., 41
Baillie, D. M., 63
Baillie, J., 35, 36
Barth, K. 15, 74
Bethune-Baker, J. F., 80
Buber, M., 13
Bultmann, R., 13, 49, 60
Butler, Bishop, 6, 24, 56

Copleston, F. C., 37–8

Ewing, A. C., 38

Farrer, A. M., 36, 37
Fuller, R. H., 61

Gentile, G., 9

Hegel, 13, 33
Hick, J., 36, 40
Hume, D., 27, 28, 40

Inge, W. R., 73

Kant, 26, 27, 33, 40, 44

Lawton, J. S., 80
Leibniz, 28
Lewis, H. D., 36, 79

Macquarrie, J., 13
Mascall, E. L., 15, 35–6, 80
Montefiore, C., 47
Moore, G. E., 25
More, P. E., 5
Mozley, J. K., 81

Nineham, D. E., 61

Origen, 10
Otto, R., 14, 17, 34

Pailin, D. A., 80
Pannenberg, W., 61
Pittenger, N., 80
Plato, 9, 14, 32, 33, 41
Plotinus, 73
Pontifex, M., 36

Ramsey, A. M., 77–8, 80
Ramsey, I. T., 37
Richardson, A., 60
Ritschl, A., 51, 66

Schleiermacher, 15, 34, 50, 52–3, 64
Sellars, R. V., 81
Smith, N. K., 37
Stout, G. F., 30, 42

Taylor, A. E., 42, 81
Temple, W., 35, 65–6, 81
Tennant, F. R., 42
Trethowan, I., 36

Underhill, E., 50

Webb, C. J., 81
Whitehead, A. N., 14, 27, 40, 59, 71

DATE DUE